Eldercare
as *Art* and *Ministry*

Irene V. Jackson-Brown

CHURCH
PUBLISHING
INCORPORATED

Unless otherwise noted, the Scripture quotations are from New Revised Standard Version Bible, copyright © 1989 National Council of the Churches of Christ in the United States of America. Used by permission. All rights reserved worldwide.

Church Publishing
19 East 34th Street
New York, NY 10016
www.churchpublishing.org

Cover design by Jennifer Kopec, 2Pug Design
Typeset by Beth Oberholtzer

A record of this book is available from the Library of Congress.

ISBN-13: 978-1-64065-307-8 (paperback)
ISBN-13: 978-1-64065-308-5 (ebook)

Contents

Acknowledgments v

Introduction Three Lives, One Calling 1

CHAPTER ONE Dolls and Nurse's Kits 7

CHAPTER TWO Caryatids and Caregivers:
The Art of Eldercare 16

CHAPTER THREE Eldercare as Ministry 21

CHAPTER FOUR The Way of Love 26

CHAPTER FIVE The Platinum Rule
of Eldercare 32

CHAPTER SIX An Ultimate Gift 36

CHAPTER SEVEN Eldercare Lingo, Skills,
and Tips 41

CHAPTER EIGHT Three Books on Compassion
and Care 70

CHAPTER NINE The High Cost of Eldercare 76

CHAPTER TEN I Don't Want to Live to Be
a Hundred! 102

CHAPTER ELEVEN Mr. Jackson's Potato Salad
and Aunt Ruth's Kale Salad 106

CHAPTER TWELVE You Don't Owe Your Loved
One Your Well-Being 110

CHAPTER THIRTEEN Stay Ready 115

Acknowledgments

Countless people nudged me to write a book that captured my learnings, experience, and problem-solving as it relates to eldercare. My father, Robert Floyd Jackson, who died in 2003 after enduring prostate cancer, paralysis, a double amputation, and all the challenges that accompany an illness, gave me my first eldercare experience. My mother, Dorothy Williams Jackson, was the quintessential nurturer, caregiver, and burden-bearer for her family; she was my first role model and passed her legacy to me. My very dear friend Marsha Bacon Glover set me on a road to professionalize my experience, urging me to seek certification as a geriatric care manager. Had my husband, Enrique, not seen an article in the local newspaper about care management, this book could not have been written.

Many medical and non-medical providers have given their endorsement and support along the way. Karole L. Thomas, RN, MSN, CHPN, and Gail Aaron, RN, then nurses at Providence Hospital in Washington, DC, wrote in 2007: "If I ever get old and need care, I'd want Irene to manage my care; she leaves no stone unturned. She is exceptional in new sensitivity and management of caregiving issues." Horace F. Greene, MD, a psychiatrist who practiced in Washington, DC, supported me in this way: "I hold case reviews with Irene. She is extremely intuitive and attends to the whole person. She is a consummate advocate. I find her most ready and equipped to provide high-quality care management." His endorsement fortified my confidence as an eldercare provider. Stephen Seabron, MD, and Hector Estepan, MD, my father's physicians through thick and thin, were models of compassion and empathy, attributes so necessary for the professional endeavor that I had no idea I would later embrace. As models, they gave me insights about care that I would not have easily encountered otherwise. My training at the Washington School of Psychiatry with Tybe Diamond, psychotherapist par excellence, and at the Washington Baltimore Center for Psychoanalysis during a yearlong fellowship, guided me toward a deeper understanding of the many dynamics—both my own and those of my clients—that are at play in eldercare as an enterprise. There are many others. I am forever grateful for their guidance, teachings, and affirmation.

I must acknowledge several clergy, many of them Episcopal priests, who gave me the injunction that I often needed to hear: to be sure to take a break and rest. A hospice chaplain, the Rev. Lawrence Sandidge was always "at the ready" to give advice and comfort to me when I faced end-of-life care for the people I served.

I am immensely indebted to the people and families who allowed me to join them along their own aging journey or the unexpected journey taken by their loved one. Countless individuals, couples, older adults, very old adults, and young adults all trusted my guidance. I thank each one for the joy that I received from serving them. There's the Jarvis family, the Browns, Grays, Edmonds, Beards, Santurios, Brooks, Nichols, Nicholsons, Quicks, Wesleys, Epps, Brown-Nolans, Dodsons, Janifers, Floyds, Edmonds, Brands, Mabuchis, Lynns, Fitzhughs, Moores, Walkers, Cyruses, Wilsons, Kecks, Tinsleys, Williamses, Fryers, Smiths, Scarboros, Paschalls, and many, many others with whom I had an intense and often complex relationship. I can only mention a few here.

There were the frontline workers without whom I could not have been as effective as I have been. These individuals stayed the course with me through countless difficult and challenging circumstances. To Waveney Luke, Delonte Downey, and Maureen Fenton, I am eternally grateful, beyond words.

Many other friends and family—despite my protestations—had no trouble telling me that it was a debt that I owed, that is, to share my experience in a book. I thank each one for their often rigorous hounding—yes, hounding. I especially appreciate my professional sidekick and friend Donna Mosley Coleman who oversees the things that I do not like to do, nor want to learn how to do. I must acknowledge my adopted goddaughter, Shelley Norfleet, who was a gift to me by helping me with my father's care.

I appreciate Lee Chavous, who owns one of the home care companies that has provided professional caregivers for my clients, often on a moment's notice. Maggie Schmidt's company also stood with me and provided the "client-specific" caregivers that I sought for someone. Once, I needed someone who was bilingual (French-English), highly educated, and world traveled as a "friendly visitor" for a ninety-year-old woman who "required" these specific attributes in a companion.

There's Beth Jansen, my sister in the profession. Beth had an early career as a social worker and a lengthy tenure as an executive at many senior living communities. She is a consummate senior-serving professional. She is always willing and ready to offer insights about particular difficult and complex care situations. Beth has been an untiring member of my "council of advisors" for years. Recently,

Beth's care team where she served as executive director gave me the title "Warrior Angel," which they considered, as do I, most accurate. Rabiat Osunsade, PA, one of the most knowledgeable and creative nurses I've ever encountered, has aided me in so many ways. We have forged a professional relationship and friendship.

When I submitted a book proposal to Nancy Bryan at Church Publishing Incorporated (CPI), I wasn't sure that there would be an interest in my proposal. There was a bit of time, I felt, before I heard from Nancy. And then came a positive response! My pages benefited from the excellent substantive editing by Milton Brasher-Cunningham and the CPI production team that brought my manuscript to fruition as a book.

My patient husband of forty-three years has endured my complete immersion in working to find solutions for the people in my care. Through Enrique, I am learning, but have not yet accomplished, the need to be the "non-anxious presence," so necessary to be effective in this work. My son, Guillermo, understands how I can be so completely absorbed in what I do that even he sometimes cannot get my attention. He forever reminds me that once when he was about eight or so, he and a friend approached me, giggling as kids do. We both happened to be in the Greenwich, Connecticut library at the same time. I was so deeply absorbed; Guillermo said that I looked at him as if I didn't recognize him and then immediately turned back to what I was doing. From him, I became aware of the intensity of my concentration. I love my men deeply, most of the time!

I hope that in these pages I captured stories as accurately as possible. And I hope that the suggestions—not advice (smile)—are helpful for all of us who face eldercare in one or several of its many forms.

INTRODUCTION

Three Lives, One Calling

I have had three professional lives, three careers, but one calling. My calling has been expressed as a teacher, mentor, consultant, lay church professional, and entrepreneur. At first glance, these callings may seem completely unrelated.

After earning my PhD in a subfield of cultural anthropology, I began a career in academe. My first "real job" was not only demanding but fraught with a lot of "isms": racism, sexism, and ageism. I was twenty-five when I started to teach at Yale as a lecturer. I was then promoted to assistant professor with the completion of my doctorate. I was married, pregnant, and young. There were few women at Yale then, even in the junior rank. I was even told when I went to the health center for prenatal care that I was the first woman on the Yale faculty to be pregnant. Whether this was true or not, I don't know. But I was an anomaly. In 1990, thirteen years after leaving Yale as a junior faculty member, I was selected as a research fellow at the Institute of Sacred Music, Worship, and the Arts at Yale Divinity School. This was made possible because of a sabbatical granted by the Episcopal Church Center.

Returning to my brief tenure at Yale, in the early 1970s, the campus was an "academic maledom"—a term I coined. I taught students who had never had a female classmate or professor. There was an unspoken and subtle bias against women, female faculty with children, and married female faculty, mixed with the usual racism against anyone other than white Anglo-Saxon Protestants. The message was clear: while I was tolerated, I was not wholly welcome.

Soon after the birth of my son, Guillermo, my undergraduate mentor, Doris McGinty (who was among the first Americans to receive a DPhil in her field from Oxford), asked me to return to Howard University to teach. I felt I owed a debt to my undergraduate alma mater, and returning to Howard would be my chance to "give back." I accepted an appointment as an associate professor and project director. And thus began a weekly commute from Stamford, Connecticut, to Washington, DC. During this time, Enrique, my husband, was busy with the founding of the Instituto Pastoral Hispano, a theological training center supported by five dioceses. So, there was a lot of juggling since our son was two years old then. Fortunately, my parents were always available to help on either end, in Washington or Connecticut. Plus, we were fortunate to have a wonderful babysitter for Guillermo, and Enrique was as active a father as he could be, so there was solid support. But this was a challenge for all of us.

At that time, commuting with a young child was nontraditional. Both Enrique and I were needled about it because it wasn't the norm back then. Even one of Enrique's colleagues, a priest, let him know that "allowing" his wife to commute to "a job" was just not right (let alone allowing her to have a hyphenated name). At Howard, the dean, in particular, seemed to support me, but I felt that he always wondered if I was serious about continuing at Howard after my initial contract expired. I suppose the dean was testing me. I certainly was testing Howard to determine if it was the setting that really felt "right." Of course, remaining at Howard would mean a move to Washington, DC. And frankly, I wasn't sure I wanted that to be the reason for a family move, even though Enrique was willing to relocate.

During my two and a half years at Howard, I was highly productive. I had all the requisite teaching experience and a track record of publications and scholarly activities for tenure track advancement to associate professor. It's always been my guess that the powers that made advancement decisions felt that I hadn't paid enough dues. I left Howard disappointed and somewhat bitter after my experiences there and at Yale, and I wondered if academe was where I wanted to spend my professional life. The game of academic life, at least as I experienced it at Yale and Howard, was not one that I wanted to play.

One evening after I left Howard, Enrique and I were invited to dinner at the home of a priest colleague. Another couple, a bishop and his wife, were also there. The bishop, the late Rt. Rev. Elliott Sorge, was an executive at the Episcopal Church Center in New York. He headed the church's Education for Mission and Ministry Unit. After dinner, while playing a game that somehow involved the *New Yorker* magazine, Bishop Sorge, who preferred to be addressed as Elliott, mentioned that he needed someone to manage the development of resources and publications in the education unit. I remember asking, "Would you be interested in adding a competent African American laywoman to your team?" I remember emphasizing both "African American" and "laywoman." There were few

African Americans at the Church Center at that time, few laity as professional staff, and few women.

Elliott was familiar with me by my reputation as a consultant to the Office of Black Ministries, a job that had been a "right person at the right time" event for me. Sometime in 1978, Frank Turner, a priest who headed the Office of Black Ministries, mentioned a hymnal project that he hoped would capture the religious song tradition of African Americans for use in the Episcopal Church and beyond. Enrique happened to be at the meeting when Frank brought up the project, and he said, "I know just the right person for the project: Irene, my wife." My dissertation and scholarly research had been focused on worship and the religious musical traditions of African Americans. I knew these traditions firsthand, having grown up in the African American cultural traditions of hymns, spirituals, and gospel music. And so began my association with the Episcopal Church Center (or 815, as it is often known) as a consultant to the Office of Black Ministries and editor of the Episcopal Church's initial publication in 1979, *Lift Every Voice and Sing*.

So, when Elliott brought me on staff at 815, it renewed an association that began with the hymnal project. I served as a lay church professional there in several capacities from 1979 to 1998.

In 1997, Enrique was called to a collaboration between the Diocese of Washington and St. John's, Lafayette Square, as vicar, Mission San Juan and Missioner for Multicultural Ministry Development. We moved from New York to Washington, DC, the place of my birth. But, for me, the return "home" was traumatic. Besides relocating my father, who was by then paralyzed, it also meant re-confronting significant life losses: my mother's death, the death of my two closest aunts, and the death of a dear friend. Little did I know then that my return to Washington would crystallize and formalize a ministry.

There are many designations that can describe what I do in the field of aging: senior-serving professional, aging life care professional, applied gerontologist, geriatric care manager, aging specialist. What I do is apply knowledge to individuals and families about issues that surround aging. My professional certifications derive from three entities: the Aging Life Care Association (formerly known as the National Association of Professional Geriatric Care Managers), the Society of Certified Senior Advisors, and the National Council of Certified Dementia Practitioners.

My most profound personal and family caregiving experience, however, has been as my father's caregiver. Many influences have helped to shape my "professionalization" as a caregiver. First, from academe I gained research and problem-solving skills, as well as the skills of a participant-observer. From my tenure at the Episcopal Church Center, an understanding of the ministry of the laity took root. My association with NTL Institute for Applied Behavioral Science as general editor of NTL's *The Reading Book for Human Relations Training, 8th Edition* introduced me to an understanding of human dynamics; my other activities as a consultant there laid the groundwork for my understanding of human behavior.

Continuing education has also enlightened and broadened my work. My most profound educational experiences were a multiyear program on aging at the Washington School of Psychiatry and a fellowship at the Washington Baltimore Center for Psychoanalysis. I must include my participation in Georgetown University's Mini-Medical School with weekly presentations by physicians for a lay audience, as well as countless continuing education courses, including a forty-hour training in basic mediation. These experiences—tools—have all been invaluable in my ministry.

CHAPTER ONE

Dolls and Nurse's Kits

My unintentional vocation as a caregiver's caregiver may well have been foreshadowed when I was a child. Is it likely that those of us who are nurturers, caregivers, are genetically imprinted for caregiving? Or are we formed? Of course, there's no certain answer to those two questions.

As a little girl, I loved playing with dolls. And I loved nurse's kits. When I was about seven, all I wanted for Christmas was a specific kind of doll: a black doll that was dressed as a bride and could walk. My adoring parents—I mean Santa—filled my request and left a black bride doll that could walk under the tree. The next Christmas, all I wanted from Santa was a nurse's kit, a popular toy for girls in the fifties. The toy kit contained a plastic stethoscope, a plastic thermometer, candy pills, and a nurse's cap. That Christmas, I remember waking up with great anticipation, hoping that Santa had remembered. After all, I knew that I had been a good little girl. I remember bolting from my bed to the Christmas tree to see if Santa had left the highly desired toy. I looked under the tree, but there was no nurse's kit. Oh, the disappointment. It stings to this day. Santa had forgotten me.

I remember my parents coming into the living room because they heard me crying. They were puzzled. I tried to speak between tears, "Santa didn't leave me anything." My father left the living room and quickly returned carrying the nurse's kit in his hands. What joy I remember.

For years after, the family story that was told and retold was that my father was not one of Santa's good helpers. Santa had asked my father to do a favor for him and put the nurse's kit under our tree so he would not be late delivering toys to all the other children. I am embarrassed to say how long I believed that family lore.

My parents, as far back as I can remember, emphasized that the commercial side of Christmas was not as important as the true meaning of Christmas. They were steadfast about not commercializing Christmas to excess. I remember many Christmases visiting my best friend's house. Christmas gifts flowed and flowed from under her tree. I would go home and tell my mother about all the toys under Beverly's tree. Time and time again, my mother stressed the "real" meaning of Christmas.

There were always holiday gatherings in our home because my mother was the family matriarch, the oldest of ten of her siblings. My mother's father died when she was fifteen. Her father—my grandfather—was found dead on the railroad tracks in Birmingham, Alabama. He was a black man in Birmingham who owned a great deal of property. My mother remembered going with him to collect rent when she was very young. The local newspaper carried an article about his death, but the article was misleading, suggesting that my grandfather had been killed by a train. According to what the family believes, he was murdered and left on the tracks because he was considered by white people to have too much power for a black man. My mother's mother died giving birth to her twelfth child, Ruth. It was then that a promise was extracted from my mother—that she look out for her siblings. Her sisters Marge and Myrtle were close to her age, but my mother, the oldest, was given the responsibility to watch out for them all. And she fulfilled that promise to her death. Both before and after I was born, many of my mother's siblings either lived with us or were under my parents' care wherever they were, away at school or in college. My mother was a "grand" caregiver.

I enjoyed Christmas as well as rehearsing my lines for the Christmas plays that were always performed at Park Road Community Church. I was fascinated watching my mother sew elaborate costumes for the plays. I was always the narrator for the play. It was also my job to practice Christmas carols on the piano. And my other holiday job was to help my mother bake cookies and cakes. Yet, in spite of the Christmas plays, presents, and merriment, I recognized from a young age that there was sadness in our home that was especially apparent at Christmas. I felt that I had to take care of my mother because of the sadness that I saw and felt from her. The only way that I knew to take care of my mother was by being a good girl. (Being good, I also thought, meant not asking for lots of toys.) Years later, through counseling and training for my calling as a caregiver's caregiver, I was able to get in touch with those Christmas feelings of sadness. What was it in me that made me know that I should care for my mother?

A fellowship at the Washington Baltimore Center of Psychoanalysis in Laurel, Maryland, and participation in a multiyear program on aging at the Washington School of Psychiatry in Washington, DC, helped me to connect the dots between my early childhood experiences and my calling as a caregiver's caregiver.

Let me offer more insight. Looking back, I see that my caregiving instinct was apparent when I was just eighteen months old. I remember sitting on my mother's lap. She was telling me that I would soon have a little brother or sister. I was an inquisitive and precocious child—so I've been told—and I asked, "Where is the baby now?"

"In my tummy," she said.

Christmas Eve, 1949. I was at home with my father, but my mother wasn't there. I remember feeling her absence, but I don't recall being told why she wasn't home with us. I don't remember being told that she was in the hospital. Regardless, I sensed that something wasn't right. My mother wasn't home, and my father wasn't his usual jovial and playful self.

On Christmas Eve of 1949, my mother gave birth to a girl. My mother came home after a few days, but I still don't remember being told that she had been in the hospital. When she did come home, the baby sister or brother that she had promised was not with her. The baby had died soon after birth. That is sadness that I continued to carry through many Christmases. After all, I had been eagerly awaiting a real doll baby to play with and care for.

Whatever lay behind my formation as a caregiver, I now believe that my ministry as a caregiver took root in childhood. Throughout my life, I have been a caregiver for my parents, family, and friends. It has been intentional and unintentional, both formal and informal.

There were other influences that shaped me as a caregiver. When I was about thirteen, my mother enrolled me in Red Cross courses. I vividly recall "Care for the Sick and Injured," "First Aid," and "What You Need to Know When You Go to the Hospital," among others. With the Red Cross training, I became a hospital volunteer, a "candy striper." Back then, as candy stripers we could do some hands-on care, such as assist with bedpans, sterilize bandages, deliver meals, change bedside water containers, and visit with the patients. I was a curious candy striper. Once I peered into an operating room while an operation was in progress. The operating doctor saw me, smiled, and turned back to his patient. Wow, that was a great thing to behold! I was comfortable moving about a hospital and among sick and injured people. I was a candy striper for several summers; I thoroughly enjoyed my responsibilities and was very proud to wear the red, white, and blue uniform.

When I was about sixteen, I became an active family caregiver. As a teenager, I had caregiving responsibilities for my mother. She had a host of medical issues throughout her adulthood. Soon after her marriage in 1939, she contracted tuberculosis and was confined to a sanatorium for a year. Back then, shame accompanied a diagnosis of that sort. My mother's tuberculosis shaped the rest of her life and subsequently shaped mine as well.

My own preteen years included ins and outs of doctors' offices and hospitals. Around age twelve, I was diagnosed with Legg-Perthes disease, an extremely painful condition of the hip joint that causes one to limp. There's also limited range of motion and restricted physical activity due to the pain. At least this is how the disease manifested for me. Treatment included a lengthy hospital stay, traction in bed, crutches, and a built-up shoe to compensate for one leg being shorter than the other. Because of Legg-Perthes disease, I know excruciating pain and how it feels to be relegated to the sidelines, looking in. And I know what it feels like to be stared at. My peers weren't kind. Adults sometimes looked at me curiously because of my built-up shoe. I contended with the disease into my twenties. As a result of having Legg-Perthes, I have heightened empathy for people experiencing physical pain and for people who are shut out and relegated to the margins because of a physical limitation or disability.

I remember an incident in high school. I was on "restricted activities" because of my hip disease. I wanted to try out for cheerleading. Despite the pain, I practiced all the cheers, even though I was trying out to be the manager of the cheerleaders. On the day of the tryouts, I was called aside and disqualified from even trying out because of being on "restricted activities." The incident angers me to this day. It would have been fair to tell me that even the manager needed to be physically fit, if it was done compassionately. The feeling of being shut out is what haunts.

When the disease first became apparent because of the pain in my hip, my mother was in the hospital. From her hospital bed, she told me to walk around. I desperately tried to hide my limp because I knew that she would be concerned. But, I could not hide my limp or the pain.

My mother was an untiring health advocate. She always said, "Get a second opinion." In those days, people rarely advocated for themselves and instead took exactly what the doctor said. My mother would say, "Try for an answer, but accept that an answer isn't always going to come." As my advocate, my mother took me to a round of doctors in Washington, DC, for an answer to my limp and pain. When their answers did not satisfy, she took me to New York City seeking a diagnosis. I was unable to walk and had to be carried. I remember being embarrassed because I had to be carried through Grand Central Station at twelve years old.

My mother's example as a health and medical advocate helped make me into a relentless advocate for the people in my care. Just recently, an administrator at an assisted living community where I have had many people as residents nicknamed me "Warrior Angel." That name seems completely fitting.

One of the most significant developments my mother celebrated was the enactment of Medicare and Medicaid in 1965. Even as a teen, I realized that Medicare greatly eased her anxiety about the cost, both financial and emotional, of getting sick. I came to realize that my mother was burdened because of her chronic health challenges. And my father's sisters—perhaps not well-intentioned—made it clear that her illnesses put a financial burden on their "baby" brother.

I spent my undergraduate years living at home. But when I left home for grad school, my father became my mother's primary caregiver. My father lived a sheltered life into adulthood. He was the youngest of four siblings; he was his parents' favorite son. His brother, Uncle Ray, was, I'm told, a "character" who did his own thing. As an adult and into marriage, my father lived only four blocks from where he was born. In contrast, my mother moved to Washington, DC, from South Carolina in her twenties. So, a marriage of a youngest son to an eldest daughter made for some of the family-of-origin dynamics that I now realize were at play.

My mother passed away when she was only sixty-eight years old. I had just reached my forty-fifth birthday. During my mother's final major surgery, from which she did not recover, I realized how, in some ways, my father had been an incompetent caregiver. While this may sound harsh, I don't mean it as a criticism, nor do I want to devalue what he was able to do—and he did a lot. But now I understand that fear gripped him, day after day. After all, he was used to being taken care of. Daily, for years, he prepared and served my mother meals, tracked her medications, attended to household chores, and drove her to and from numerous appointments. In the process, he neglected and overlooked his own care. During the surgery, my father had a significant emotional breakdown and started to cry hysterically in the hospital's surgical waiting room.

My father blurted out, "Momma won't make it." He called my mother "Momma," a common practice among some husbands at that time. "She won't make it through the surgery, she just won't," he wailed.

In that moment, with my mother in surgery and my father breaking down, I knew I could no longer be their child. In hindsight, it was a transformational event—an emerging from childhood to adulthood. That moment propelled me full tilt into eldercare.

A few years after my mother's death, my father was diagnosed with prostate cancer. He became paralyzed because the cancer metastasized to his spine. He eventually became a double amputee because of peripheral artery disease. As a result, my father required long-term "custodial care," as it is called. And I became my father's family caregiver.

I was a solo caregiver, like most family caregivers are. And I held many pity-poo parties until my geriatric care manager told me that as an "only" I didn't have to negotiate with siblings. That was eye-opening. I was also a solo family caregiver for my father's two older sisters who never had any children; I was it. I had expected my mother's youngest sister, who lived in a nearby state, to be helpful, but she was not available to the extent that I needed her, even though my parents had been her surrogate parents. I was angry with her at first because she didn't step up as I thought she should. Looking back, I know for whatever reason, she wasn't equipped in the way that I needed her to be.

From my mother's death in 1992 to my father's death in 2003, I shouldered my father's care. Through steadfast faith and support from my husband, Enrique, and son, Guillermo, my close friend Marsha, and the many medical and non-medical professionals who helped me, along with members of the Spinal Cord Injury Network, I embraced the daunting role of full-blown eldercare.

CHAPTER TWO

Caryatids and Caregivers
The Art of Eldercare

The Fifth Avenue façade of the Metropolitan Museum of Art in New York City was finished in 1902. On the façade of the building are four niches, which were intended to house statues. They remained unfilled until 2019—for 117 years—when Wangechi Mutu, a visual artist who creates collages, videos, sculptures, and performances, was commissioned to create sculptures to fill the museum's niches in preparation for a gala event.

Mutu was born in Kenya and educated at Cooper Union (bachelor of fine arts) and Yale (graduate degree in sculpture). Her work is symbolic, representational, complex, and challenging to access. I met Wangechi through my son, Guillermo, who is a multidisciplinary performing artist and musician. They collaborated on a performance piece and have a solid friendship. Wangechi is Guillermo's older, wiser, and adopted sister. From their association and friendship, I was introduced to her paintings, which raged, to my eyes, with complex symbols, images, cultural references, and found objects—some understood, and others puzzling.

The event at the Metropolitan Museum included a public conversation with Wangechi in the Met's auditorium, which was completely filled. She explained that while the physical creation of the sculptures took a few months shy of a year, many years of envisioning, sketching, researching, and studying informed the final sculptures. She captured the cultural traditions of which she is a part, both Western and African.

Each statue in the museum's façade is a female figure draped in folds of cloth. In her talk, Wangechi explained how she worked with her hands to achieve a particular facial expression—the eyes, the turn of the head, the placement of the mirrored disc on each statue's head, among other details—before casting the figures. She elaborated about the bronzing process, as well as how and why she wanted to achieve a certain patina and coloration.

Wangechi's four statues are examples of the fluidity of the artistic process. While the final form is static, the fixed nature of the statues grew out of an organic, dynamic, and highly complex process. As an artist, she made the parts, the many processes, into a whole.

Wangechi referred to her sculptures as "caryatids." Since college, I have had a keen interest in art history and music history; yet, I do not recall encountering the word "caryatid" in my art history courses. A caryatid, from the Greek, is the name given to an architectural column that is in the form of a standing female figure. The sculpted figure takes the place of a plain column or a pillar that holds a building up. The weight of the building rests on the figure's head.

As Wangechi spoke, I thought about how caregivers, the majority of whom are women, are human caryatids. I could not help but draw the parallel between caryatids and female caregivers; both of them are essential burden-bearers. It is wondrous how one experience can stir our imagination to connect seemingly disparate things. My former colleague and dear friend Harold T. Lewis, a retired priest, says essential people "bear the burden in the heat of the day." Caregivers, like caryatids, are burden-bearers.

The late Wesley "Wes" Frensdorff, who was the bishop of the Diocese of Nevada from 1972 to 1985, was a needlepoint artist who created designs from multicolored threads. Frensdorff used the metaphor of a tangled skein of threads as the title for one of his essays. From the mash-up of threads, he fashioned a visual delight. Like Wangechi, Frensdorff used source material—for him it was colored threads—to create something visually pleasing.

Eldercare is art. Eldercare is the weaving together of separate threads—legal, medical, health, financial, spiritual—to fashion a quality of life, despite the circumstances of disease, disability, or aging. Eldercare is molding and shaping, like Wangechi did to create her sculptures. Effective eldercare is a creative endeavor, fluid and improvisational.

To be an effective eldercare provider, one must be prepared to change course, explore what is unseen, be comfortable with ambiguity, and be willing to struggle, yet never give in to frustration or despair. It is the improvisatory nature of eldercare that makes eldercare an art.

Caring for an aging loved one requires creativity. What if I am not creative, one might wonder? How, then, can I become an effective eldercare-giver? Creativity, to me, is using one's imagination; thinking in new and different ways; being innovative; being resourceful by looking at a problem from a new perspective. Creativity is coming up with a new idea. Creativity is the repurposing of a found object. Creativity is making banana bread from over-ripe bananas. Creativity is the ability to envision beyond the obvious.

Eldercare in the midst of the coronavirus pandemic is forcing families responsible for an older loved one to rely on creative problem-solving and approaches to care. I'm currently working with a couple whose daughters live three thousand miles away. Their care was daily calls and frequent visits. They relied on their father as the family caregiver for their mother, who has advanced dementia. The daughters recently learned that both parents were infected with the COVID-19 virus. Ordinarily, they would fly to their parents when there was a need. But flying in the midst of the pandemic wasn't advisable. There was a care arrangement that had been in place for over a year: 24/7 care, two shifts of twelve hours each. The agency staffed six caregivers per week. That meant twenty-eight footprints in and out of the house each week! There's little doubt that the virus was carried in, as neither member of the couple had been outside and about in months. Suddenly, and without notice, the homecare company pulled the caregivers from the home because the couple tested positive, which would have left the couple unattended. Fortunately, I had done some creative problem-solving in anticipation that the husband (and wife) would test positive for the virus and that the homecare agency would drop the case.

As the pandemic engulfs people with less than robust immune systems, ways of care have to be reimagined in service of eldercare. One example: Medicare has revised an aspect of coverage. Now physicians can bill for in-home visits and telemedicine consultations, a very recent development because of the virus. Companies that offer home-delivered, prepared meals are emerging. Some offer a full range of options, from a pureed menu to diet-specific menus.

Eldercare is art fashioned from creative thinking, exploration, and divorcing oneself from the thinking, "We've always done it that way."

CHAPTER THREE

Eldercare as Ministry

The word "ministry" can mean many things depending on context. The word can be misunderstood, or its meaning lost even when the context is known. In both secular and faith-based settings, I often open my presentation with a question, not intended to be rhetorical: "How many ministers are present?" If anyone answers affirmatively, it's usually ordained clergy. I then ask the question another way: "How many of you care in some way for an aging loved one?" Still, only a few hands are raised. These two opening questions are meant to establish a framework for understanding ministry as a responsibility, particularly of Christians; the second question is intended to broaden the understanding of eldercare as well.

Consider this: the word "eldercare" has only been in use since 1960, a mere five years before Medicare was passed. Merriam-Webster's definition is limited and outdated: "The care of older adults and especially the care of an older parent by a son or daughter." Prior to 1965, when Medicare was passed, nearly thirty states had a familial responsibility law that required an adult child to be responsible for their parents' necessities of life. Although rarely enacted, the law was used in 2012 when a nursing home won a court case that forced an adult son to pay his mother's nursing bill. Ethicist Daniel Callahan explored the question of filial responsibility in an article, "Ethics and the Care of the Elderly," published in April 1985 by the Hastings Center. It looks at the biblical injunction that children should honor their father and mother, and the extent to which an adult child is obligated to a parent.

Early in my professional work, a ninety-year-old woman who was a member of the Episcopal parish where my husband was interim rector asked me for my assistance, which I gave. Eventually, a member of her family asked me how I was helping her aunt. I explained that my work as a senior-serving professional was a ministry. A grand mess ensued. The family member called the diocese and reported to the bishop that I was raising money for my husband's parish. Then they took me to court in an effort to try to prove that I was exploiting their loved one. That unpleasantness gave me real insight about how misunderstood the word "ministry" can be.

My working definition of ministry is an "activity." Christians, in particular, are called to carry out ministry. A minister attends to the needs of another person. Giving to and helping another person were values that were inculcated in me by my parents and Sunday school teachers. Year after year, the parable of the talents was part of the Christian education curriculum. When I was twelve years old I was surprised to be given a check—my first check—for $12.50 for playing the piano for Vacation Bible School. I had to be dissuaded from returning the check because, in my mind, I was sharing and using my God-given talent, my ability to play the piano. To this day, I continue to struggle with being compensated for the ministry that I do.

Throughout my childhood, my parents and I were active in a nondenominational church, Park Road Community Church in Washington, DC. The worship there was in the black folk tradition. At Park Road, my father was superintendent of the Sunday school for years and my mother directed the Christmas, Thanksgiving, and Easter plays for the Sunday school.

During my teens, my mother returned to her Presbyterian roots and took my father and me along. At the Church of the Redeemer, Presbyterian USA, I was an active youth leader. It was a church that invited the social activists for racial justice of that time. During the summers I attended Presbyterian leadership camps. Another activity in high school was an additional way to experience Christian life, when I was a member of the Christian youth fellowship that met weekly. In college, I was active in campus ministry and regularly attended chapel, where I heard great preachers and theologians such as Benjamin Mays. Later, as junior faculty at Yale, I was active in the Black Church at Yale, which was led by seminarians. There, I founded and directed its first choir.

As an adult, I was formally introduced to the Episcopal Church by my husband. We met when he was a seminarian at Yale Divinity School. We married. Our son was born and was baptized by a priest, and I was confirmed. I was very serious about what the catechism instructed and I was struck by a particular question and answer:

Question: Who are the ministers of the Church?

Answer: The ministers of the Church are lay persons, bishops, priests, and deacons.[1]

---

1. The Book of Common Prayer, 855.

It would be later in my work as a lay church professional at the Episcopal Church Center that I began to fully understand what it means to be a "minister." We are called to ministry by baptism. As Christ's representatives in the world, we are called to exercise ministry. And ministry is exercised in daily life, in work, at leisure, in the community, and in the life of the church.

During my tenure at the Episcopal Church's headquarters, one of my responsibilities was to support the Office of Ministry Development with educational resources and publications. I was the founding editor of the *Ministry Development Journal*, a quarterly publication that had a wide circulation in the Episcopal Church during the 1980s. The publication contained articles intended to reshape, rethink, and reimagine conventional notions of ministry, working to show that ministry was not the sole providence of ordained people. Ministry is carried out by all of the members of the body of Christ, both lay and ordained.

I had frequent ah-ha moments about ministry as I began to realize that some of my daily activities, both professional and personal, were indeed ministry. For example, I now recognize the essentialness of the ministry of hospitality, whether at home or elsewhere. When my husband Enrique was archdeacon, I would sometimes accompany him to various parishes in the region he served. Far too often, I remember feeling ill at ease during coffee hour at these parishes. I didn't expect preferential treatment, but I can recall time and time again not exactly feeling any authentic hospitality, even though we are quick to say, "The Episcopal Church *welcomes you*."

In my ministry as a professional caregiver and caregiver's caregiver, exercising the ministry of presence is an essential role. Being fully present to an aging, frail, or sick person—listening, visiting, showing empathy, consoling, laughing, crying, and joking—is among the many ways of engaging in a ministry of presence. And over the past nearly twenty years, I have "skilled-up" to become more effective in carrying out a ministry of presence.

CHAPTER FOUR

The Way of Love

There are many ways to think about what it means to be old and aging. The great baseball player Satchel Paige put it this way: "How old would you be if you didn't know how old you really are?" Gerontologists have developed a rather clunky classification that is still a somewhat useful way to distinguish the range of "oldness." There is the "young-old," the "middle-old," and the "old-old." You can decide for yourself where you may or may not fit. I would like to insert another class: "pre-old," similar to "preteen."

I was "pre-old" in my forties (smile), and in the middle of a sabbatical as a research fellow at Yale Divinity School's Institute of Sacred Music, Worship, and the Arts, when the trajectory of my life changed drastically. My unintended journey as a bona fide, unprepared, frightened, overwhelmed, and conflicted caregiver began. I had a robust professional life, I was the mother of a gifted young son, and I was a clergy wife whose husband had responsibility for nearly seventy parishes as an archdeacon.

In the middle of it all, Enrique read an article in the newspaper about a senior-serving professional. The article mentioned an emerging resource to help families navigate the maze of eldercare. The article featured Lenise Dolen, PhD, a psychologist/gerontologist. Years later, the September 30, 2018, obituary in the *New York Times* credited her as a pioneer in the field of eldercare and a founding member of the Aging Life Care Association (formerly the National Association of Professional Geriatric Care Managers). After reading the article Enrique had found, I immediately made an appointment with her. That was around 1992. Subsequently, she guided me through the most difficult early challenges with my father after his cancer diagnosis, including his new needs as a paraplegic. It was her guidance and support and my growing understanding of the ministry of the laity that helped me learn how to begin to climb the rough side of a mountain as my father's caregiver.

The Way of Love

The presiding bishop of the Episcopal Church, Michael Curry, has offered a Rule of Life called "The Way of Love." A Rule of Life is an ancient practice that involves an intentional commitment to a set of practices that provide guidance, rhythm, and inspiration for living a meaningful life. Bishop Curry defines seven steps on the Way of Love: turn, learn, pray, worship, bless, go, and rest. Though not all of the steps are applicable, I find much of the Way of Love also serves as a Rule of Life for eldercare.

- **Go:** Jesus sends us to move and to go beyond our circles of comfort. Eldercare is disquieting and uncomfortable. We must act, often when we are not ready or do not feel equipped.

- **Bless:** Jesus empowers us and has blessed us, as Jesus did the disciples, to serve with time, talents, and treasure. Eldercare requires all three: patience is another way of naming our time; we have an opportunity to discern and use our gifts; and as caregivers, we often must supplement the cost of care for our loved ones.

- **Rest:** How do we find the time to be still when eldercare responsibilities are front and center? Remember the Sabbath. We are permitted to "be still." We must do nothing. It is probably the greatest challenge for a caregiver. I stumbled on the phrase "holy busyness"; it is a far too easy default setting. As caregivers, we can easily become the consummate "suffering servant," the one who suffers "without cause." It is easy to become "an instrument of our own oppression," as my friend and guide the Rev. Earl Neil would say.

- **Learn:** Growth is essential for a caregiver. We must listen to the experiences of other caregivers and benefit from their stories. The Bible gives us examples of how God acts and cares. In the many homilies and presentations that I have given over the years, I have often turned to the powerful story about Simon Peter's mother-in-law, who was sick and needed a caregiver. The story goes that Jesus touched her—gave her care. The woman got up and cared for the people who had gathered by preparing a meal. Learning to be a caregiver comes experientially by "doing care" undergirded by knowledge.

- **Turn:** Often during an initial assessment and consultation, I hear about an older loved one's behavior: they wander, forget, look unkempt, smell, drive erratically, and so on. Yet, the family caregiver's denial obfuscates the real cause of the behaviors, which may be dementia. Eldercare requires turning from denial to acceptance. Caregiving requires turning from apathy to empathy. It means turning the emphasis from cure to care, turning from diagnosis and disease to the loved one's emotional and spiritual needs.

The way I learned to live into this Rule of Life was through caring for people.

Mrs. Lucas

In my presentations about eldercare, I often start by asking, "How many people in the room are caregivers for an older loved one?" Usually, only a few people raise a hand. The goal of my presentations is to change the way attendees think about caregiving and about themselves as caregivers. Caregiving, I point out, can be intermittent, intense, short- or long-term.

I grew up in a neighborhood where everyone knew each other. I was one of the youngest children on the street. I had playmates, but they lived around the corner, a few blocks from me. Our house was directly across the street from Mrs. Lucas's. I was probably around eight years old when my mother told me that she wanted me to start visiting Mrs. Lucas. She seemed very old to me. Ancient. She had scraggly hair that she wore in two long braids. She was very thin. And she was the same height as I was. She had a particular odor, which was not unpleasant, just distinctive. Her house smelled the same way that she did.

My mother insisted that I visit Mrs. Lucas weekly. I would cross the street, and she would open the door right away as though she knew that it was me. Sometimes, she would ask me to run an errand. Looking back now as an adult, I'm pretty sure that my mother asked Mrs. Lucas to send me on errands to help instill values of responsibility and reliability in me. Since I had no grandparents who were alive, I imagined Mrs. Lucas as my grandmother. I loved visiting. I remember being captivated by her stories from the "olden days." And she gave me treats, also to my delight. As I think back, caring for Mrs. Lucas was my first step on the way to becoming an eldercare-giver.

Harry

"How many clients do you have?" I am often asked, which makes me curious about what the inquirer is trying to determine. Do people typically ask an attorney or other solo practitioner how many clients they have? Whatever the reason for asking, I use the question as a teachable moment by answering, "Caring for an aging loved one involves a gaggle of relationships." Eldercare is not about one person. The gaggle of relationships is called a "client system," to use professional jargon. Its members are related to one another, but ultimately the recipient of the care is "the client."

It is foundational to understand that caregiving is an intimate relationship. At the same time, it is not one-to-one because caregiving must involve a host of other people. Often, I find that family caregivers fail to recognize the gaggle of relationships and become overwhelmed because of the complexity of it all. I often say to family caregivers, "It is not possible to dip your toes in at the edge of the water; eldercare requires plunging into the water with your entire body."

Harry (not his real name) was a client in his early seventies. He had a complicated diagnosis that included cognitive impairment. I believe that he had been stigmatized. His medical record included what, I discovered, was erroneous documentation. He had lived first in his apartment and later in a small group home before I became his professional caregiver. His health had declined and his quality of life had deteriorated by the time I was called in to help. He had problems walking; his gait was unsteady. He had an eye injury and was legally blind. According to the consulting neurologist, Harry had all the indications for NPH (normal pressure hydrocephalus). Often mistaken for a form of dementia, NPH's manifestations are problems with walking and bladder control, and difficulty thinking and reasoning. NPH is acquired in adulthood. For Harry, his hydrocephalus may well have been caused by a head injury. Harry had neglected his own care for years.

It required nearly a year of active care management to improve Harry's health and quality of life. I coordinated his care with a team that included a primary care physician, a cardiologist, a neurologist, a psychiatrist, a radiologist, two ophthalmologists with separate specialties, a dermatologist, a podiatrist, a dentist, professional caregivers, and nurses. I also managed relationships with his family, friends, city and federal governmental agencies, a transportation company, a home health agency, a hospital, an assisted living community, and his church. This is an example of the gaggle of relationships I mentioned earlier.

Be prepared. Effective caregiving requires continuous coordination—back and forth, over and over, and again and again.

CHAPTER FIVE

The Platinum Rule of Eldercare

"Treat others the way that you would want to be treated" is the golden rule. A version of this is what I call the "platinum rule of caregiving": "Treat others the way *they* want to be treated." To the extent possible, put yourself in the care receiver's shoes and treat them accordingly. To do so requires empathy on the caregiver's part. And it requires putting aside what we, as caregivers, think is right and entering the care recipient's world.

While I was writing this book, I was contacted by a fellow professional geriatric care manager who was completing research about microaggressions that occur in caregiving. The researcher and aging life care professional/geriatric care manager, Kim Kozina-Evanoski, LMSW, CMC, CDP, EdD, was collecting data for her dissertation from St. John Fisher College and asked to interview me. Her research study, "Professional Perceptions of Microaggressions and Verbal Abuse toward Aged Women," looked at micro-aggressions from caregiver toward care receiver, or medical provider toward patient. At first, I could not think of an example that I had encountered. Since microaggressions are subtle, they can go unrecognized. A microaggression is a subtle verbal, behavioral, or environmental indignity, whether intentional or unintentional, that communicates slights and insults from one person to another.

After some thought and prompting from Kim, I thought of a former client, Alice, now deceased. When I met Alice, she lived in her own home. She was always neat in appearance, manicured, and well-dressed. At ninety-two, she walked the two blocks to her hair salon weekly. Her hair was always groomed in a stylish cut. When she was no longer able to live independently, she was moved to a nursing home by her guardian-conservator. When I happened to visit the nursing home where she had been for three years, I saw her, diminished and infantilized. Her hair was plaited in small braids, childlike, all over her head. The infantilization that was imposed on her was, in my view, a microaggression.

Effective caregiving requires a particular kind of competency—emotional intelligence, empathy—that includes putting aside one's own notions in service to the other person's needs and desires.

An emotionally intelligent and sensitive caregiver, Beth—who is and has been an executive director of assisted living communities in the Washington, DC, area—is an example of one who exemplifies the needed skills (and talents) for effective caregiving. Ann was a resident at Beth's assisted living community. Ann's son lived eight hours away, so he was only able to visit his mother sporadically. Beth had referred him to me, and he asked me to keep an eye on his mother. I did so for months when I visited the assisted living community where she lived.

Ann always wore pearls, lipstick, blush, false eyelashes, and coordinated ensembles. She had a wardrobe of wigs, all quite glamorous in styling. When it came time for Ann to move to be closer to her son, I was responsible for her relocation. I wanted to make sure that the staff at what was to be her new assisted living community would know exactly how Ann liked to look in terms of her personal appearance. During the admission process, I told the staff that Ann wore false eyelashes. The admissions director at the new facility asked if Ann applied the eyelashes herself.

"No," I said. "Each morning, Beth takes time away from her work as executive director to apply Ann's eyelashes." Beth went well beyond the scope of what one would think of as caregiving. Beth understood Ann's need to wear false eyelashes. That is who Ann was before living with dementia. Ann didn't *have* to have false eyelashes applied daily; it wasn't essential to her health. But wearing eyelashes maintained her self-esteem and underscored who she was before she lived with dementia. I do not know whether Ann's new community had anyone who was as sensitive to Ann as Beth had been in terms of how Ann wanted to look. I doubt it. Wearing eyelashes enhanced Ann's quality of life. Effective and loving caregiving is the willingness to put our own notions of what is essential in the background. It's easy to say, hard to do.

I had lunch with three ladies at an assisted living community where I have several clients. Each one was "present" in her own way. Here's what I observed. Pat asked the server for a turkey sandwich. The server asked, "What kind of bread do you want?" Pat answered, "Toasted." Pat has difficulty using utensils because of Parkinson's disease. Pat's sandwich was served with soft bread, not toasted as she had ordered. The soft bread made it difficult for her to pick up and hold the sandwich. I watched the sandwich fall apart as she struggled to hold it together to eat it.

Another resident at the lunch table ordered what she wanted from the menu. When her meal was delivered, she just looked at the plate and picked at the food, rather than eating it. Observing this, I asked, "You're not eating. Do you want to order something else?"

"No," she answered. "I just don't want so much food on my plate at one time."

The third resident at our table had also ordered a turkey sandwich. I noticed that she seemed not to be enjoying her lunch. I asked, "Is the sandwich fixed the way you like it?"

She answered hesitantly, "Yes, it's okay." I probed a little more to discover that she had asked for mayonnaise on the sandwich. Instead, her sandwich had mustard on it.

Juan, the dining room chef, makes a round during meals to check on dining residents. When he came to our table and asked if everything was okay, they all answered, "Fine," in unison, which was not the case. I spoke up for each of the women, pointing out that their food had not been served the way they had ordered it.

Caregiving is advocacy—speaking up on behalf of the person who requires care. Caregiving is being fully present, observing and listening for the unspoken. Far too often, care receivers are compliant, especially if they must depend on a caregiver. In many ways, care receivers feel powerless and simply give in. Each one of the women thanked me for speaking up on their behalf. But they also realized that Juan listened to each one of them and promised to pay better attention to how their meals were prepared and served in the future. Juan promised to use a version of the platinum rule of caregiving: respect the person, ask what they want, and then give it to them to the extent possible and without harm.

CHAPTER SIX

An Ultimate Gift

Eldercare takes many forms. An eldercare-giver can be an activist, advocate, nurturer, helper, organizer, observer, questioner, entertainer, problem-solver, investigator, peacemaker, coordinator, and researcher, to cite a few roles.

W. Steven Carter, a participant in the 2005 White House Conference on Aging, proposed, "[There is] no cohesive theology of aging that exists to define values and roles of elders and those caring for and responding to them." Carter urged that local and regional centers be developed to train, support, and counsel family caregivers. He further recommended that churches should ensure appropriate recognition of and response to the spiritual, emotional, and psychological needs of caregivers. This was a clarion call to congregations.

In 2001, at a Duke University conference, "Faith in the Future: Religion, Aging, and Healthcare in the 21st Century," the late bioethicist Daniel Callahan spoke to the question, "Caring: What does it really mean?" He examined the imbalance in our society between *curing* and *caring*, with lesser societal support for caring. He pointed out that the imbalance will become more dramatic as the elderly *live* with chronic illnesses that cannot be *cured*.

Callahan went on to offer a most poignant reflection: "Caring is an art and the ultimate gift from one special person to another who can no longer provide for him or herself." A. Wayne Schwab, in his book *When the Members Are the Missionaries: An Extraordinary Calling for Ordinary People*, puts forth an understanding of where people can be called to be a missionary—at home, at work, in the local community, in the wider world, at leisure, and in the church. Eldercare is an explicit opportunity for the laity to minister in a specific mission field: the home.

My thinking about "the mission field" has been enlarged, particularly through working with Reverend Schwab on his book. He emphasizes "the missions of each of the baptized" and includes the home as a mission field.[1]

A publication, "A Study of Religion, Ministry, and Meaning in Caregiving Among Health Professionals in an Institutional Setting in New York City," published in the *Journal of Pastoral Care & Counseling,* surveyed the religious practices of the staff of a large New York nursing home.[2] Respondents were asked about the degree to which they saw their work as a ministry and the meaning they obtained from being caregivers. The survey concluded that for those who were "religious," religiosity appeared to enhance the meaning the caregiving staff received from their work.

Also notable is a study, "Religion and the Meaning of Work," published in the *Journal for the Scientific Study of*

1. A. Wayne Schwab, *When the Members Are the Missionaries: An Extraordinary Calling for Ordinary People* (Essex, NY: Member Mission Press, 2002), 3.

2. Jon A. Overvold et al., "A Study of Religion, Ministry, and Meaning in Caregiving Among Health Professionals in an Institutional Setting in New York City," *Journal of Pastoral Care & Counseling* 59, no. 3 (September 1, 2005): 225–35.

Religion, that surveyed over 3,400 members of more than 30 Protestant and Catholic congregations.[3] The study tested the hypothesis that the more "religious" an individual was, the more they saw their work as a calling or ministry, as opposed to a job. In all, 15 percent of those surveyed agreed with the statement, "My work has special meaning because I have been called to do what I'm doing regardless of how much time it takes or how little money I have; I was put on earth to do what I am doing."[4]

An individual who provides care for an adult loved one or bears caregiving responsibilities often does not recognize himself or herself as a "caregiver." Caregiving is central in the ministry of Jesus. Scripture makes it clear that caregiving is central to the Church's life and that we are called to care for one another. And caring for God's people is not the exclusive responsibility of the *ordained* ministers.

Society undervalues caregiving and caregivers, and religious bodies continue to do too little in being intentional about equipping the laity for this ministry. Evidence suggests that religious bodies provide little support, training, and even affirmation of eldercare-giving as a ministry.

Christians are fully authorized, by baptism, to do ministry in the world. "Lay people," as the late theologian Verna Dozier wrote, "become weary of the struggle and give over the responsibility to ecclesiastical hierarchy."[5] Ordained ministers must enable the laity to fulfill their peculiar, inalienable ministry and equip them for their primary function—to be servants *in the world*. I want to lift high the authority of the

---

3. J. C. Davidson and D. P. Caddell, "Religion and the Meaning of Work," *Journal for the Scientific Study of Religion* 33, no. 2: 135–47.

4. Davidson and Caddell, "Religion and the Meaning of Work," 138.

5. Cynthia L. Shattuck and Fredrica Harris Thompsett, eds., *Confronted by God: The Essential Verna Dozier* (New York: Seabury, 2006), 67.

laity as they carry out a ministry of eldercare where Jesus can be made manifest. We follow Christ as we provide care.

Gift Given, Gift Received

Caregiving touches all of us. A paraphrase of former first lady Rosalyn Carter's wise words sums this up.

There are only four kinds of people in the world:

1. People who have given care;
2. People who are giving care;
3. People who will be giving care;
4. People who will need care.

Giving the gift of care requires thoughtfulness. And receiving the gift of care with gratefulness and appreciation is not necessarily apparent to the gift giver.

Here's what I mean. "How To" books have been plentiful for years. In my teens, my mother gave me a copy of *Amy Vanderbilt's Complete Book of Etiquette*. When it was published in 1952, it was touted as "the most authoritative book of its kind," according to the description of the book on Amazon. I remember how annoyed I was when I received that gift. I was not grateful. Yet, I did a similar thing with my son and other young family members and friends when I gifted them an instruction book of good and proper etiquette. I gave them each a copy of a little blue book called *Tiffany's Table Manners for Teenagers* (March 18, 1989). They were not appreciative.

Instruction and "How To" books for caregivers are a recent phenomenon. I don't remember there being a book on caregiving "etiquette" or instruction when I began my caregiving journey. I certainly could have used such a resource and guidance. The guidance eventually came in the form of a geriatric care manager, the late Dr. Denise Dolan, a psychologist who was among the few aging specialists in the still relatively new field of geriatric care management in 1992. The first professional association for this field was created in 1985 as the National Association of Professional Geriatric Care Managers, now called the Aging Life Care Association (ALCA, www.aginglife care.org).

ALCA has grown over the decades since its inception. However, the benefits of using a geriatric care manager remain relatively untapped. Geriatric care managers are aging experts and offer knowledge, best practices, and a hand to hold to guide a family in caring for and preparing to care for an older loved one.

CHAPTER SEVEN

Eldercare Lingo, Skills, and Tips

Every enterprise or activity has a unique lingo and alphabet soup of acronyms, abbreviations, phrases, and shorthand. Caregiving has its own panoply of phrases and words that are often confusing at best. A recent chat with a colleague illustrates how subtle and confusing the language of health care and hence eldercare is. My colleague was affiliated with a hospice organization, but she was considering a move to a company that provided *home health services.*

I asked, "So, what's your hourly rate for CNAs (certified nursing aides)?" She looked at me, puzzled.

She said, "Irene, we don't staff CNAs, we're a *home health company,* not *a home care company.*" She went on to point out the difference between the two, which I readily understood. But here's the point. In my many years of family and professional eldercare, as the eldercare-giver's caregiver, I, too, sometimes misunderstand the subtleties in the industry.

A home *health* company provides services such as in-home physical and occupational therapy, other needed short-term services after a hospital stay, short-term home visits by a nurse, and durable medical equipment. Typically, home *health* companies are reimbursed by Medicare and are not dependent on private pay.

A home *care* company can be an agency or a registry. It's important for caregivers to know the difference between an agency versus a registry. An agency employs its staff; a registry typically uses contract workers or independent contractors. Be sure to ask the company you're contacting for home support if they're an agency or a registry. Home *care* companies typically do not staff drivers, maids, cleaning people, cooks, childcare providers, and so forth.

Essential to being an effective eldercare provider is having an understanding, even if only basic, of the language of eldercare. Following are some phrases, words, and acronyms that are en vogue and are the ABCs of eldercare. I have encountered countless highly educated professionals, attorneys for example, who are ill-informed or lack a basic understanding of these terms. The explanations for the terms offered here are very basic and my own.

24/7 or round-the-clock care: Widely misunderstood. Usage varies, depending on how the phrase is used and by whom. Twenty-four-hour care signals that a person requires continuous "care." It does not necessarily mean that a person requires continuous, unceasing care. Be advised: 24/7 "care" can be a combination of assistance, oversight, monitoring, and hands-on care. It does not necessarily mean that the person requires one-to-one care in a "facility" such as a nursing home or assisted living community. Yet, 24/7 is often presented as if it means one-to-one care by a care professional. The phrase has become a "shorthand" way, albeit a misleading one, to indicate that a person requires "care," but it does not necessarily mean one paid professional caregiver to one "patient."

Be advised: when a home care agency is told that a person requires 24/7 care, this usually will mean two shifts (two different aides) working twelve hours each. This staffing by a professional caregiver is paid by the hour and is private pay. Medicare does not cover one-to-one care.

I panicked when I was told that my father would require 24/7 care upon his discharge from the acute rehab hospital where he had been a patient for months. It was then that I was told that a nursing home would be the only option for the level of care he needed. Wrong! Wrong! Wrong! It was my own geriatric care manager, Lenise Dolan, who developed a plan of care, arranged my father's rescue from the nursing home, and helped me to coordinate care at home that included a combination of care providers, paid caregivers, volunteers, family, and friendly visitors.

Know that continuous one-to-one care is not provided in any setting, except in the ICU; one-to-one care is not provided in an assisted living setting or even in a nursing home. An article in the *New York Times*, February 14, 2020, "Some Assisted-Living Residents Don't Get Promised Care," is worth citing about staffing ratios, including the fact that only nineteen states specify a minimum staffing ratio at all.[1] My experience has been that long-term communities, whether a small or large assisted living facility or even a nursing home, set high expectations in this regard; a resident's loved one is overwhelmed during the admission process and doesn't track, hear, or understand that there is a staff to resident ratio of something like ten to one during the day and even higher during the

---

1. Paula Span, "Some Assisted-Living Residents Don't Get Promised Care, Suit Charges," *New York Times*, February 14, 2020, https://www.nytimes.com/2020/02/14/health/assisted-living-staffing.html.

night. The family's expectation of care coverage is often way out of line with the reality. This is why having a geriatric care manager as part of the loved one's team can help present the reality of staff to resident ratio.

I recall my own misunderstanding when my father was admitted to an assisted living community in Connecticut where he stayed for a few weeks before I discovered a geriatric care manager. I remember visiting the place in Greenwich that I was considering for my father and I saw many residents with attendants sitting close by. Naively, I assumed that those residents were being attended by staff. Yet, to my mind, it was reasonable, since the monthly cost for that facility in the early 1990s was over $8,000. However, I was shocked when I later was told by my geriatric care manager, our advocate, that the "sitters" were privately paid aides and not staff.

Acute vs. sub-acute care: Acute care is provided in a hospital. Yet, a visit to the emergency room of a hospital may or may not constitute an admission, even if the person is assigned a bed. As an advocate for your loved one, ask, and get a firm answer, what your loved one's status is—whether admission or observation. Do not assume that because your loved one is given a bed that he or she has actually been admitted. This is all about Medicare reimbursement to the hospital. Now, Medicare requires at least a three-day admission, not observation status, in order for admission to a sub-acute facility for rehab. Sub-acute care is speech, occupational, or physical therapy. Sub-acute care, also known as rehab, can be delivered in different settings. A rehab company can come to your loved one's home. Or, outpatient rehab can be provided at a freestanding entity, or provided in a nursing home as sub-acute care.

Inpatient rehab at a nursing home is delivered by a separate rehab company that is contracted by the nursing home. Therefore, there are two separate entities housed under the same roof. In this arrangement, rehab services are delivered by the rehabilitation provider and care is delivered by the nursing staff.

A little-known option is also available: some assisted-living communities have a sub-acute rehab company embedded in the building. In this arrangement, Medicare covers rehab (short-term) and private pay covers the care and services provided by the assisted living community. (A note: assisted living communities are now offering a respite stay or short-term stays of several months while a person receives rehab or recovers from a hospital stay before returning home. This is a separate pricing structure from someone admitted to an assisted living community for a permanent stay.)

AD: Alzheimer's disease, the most widely known and most common of dementias. The mistake that is often made is that other forms of dementia go unrecognized and the diagnosis becomes AD.

ADLs: Activities of daily living refer to eating, bathing, dressing, ambulating, and so on. A person requiring care is assigned the degree of care required: "some assistance," "total assistance," and "standby assistance." For example, a person may need some assistance with eating, but total assistance with bathing and dressing. Most long-term care insurance policies require that a person needs assistance with at least two ADLs, but this can vary.

Aging-in-place: A plan of care and essentially a movement in eldercare with the goal of enabling the care receiver to remain in their choice of residence. This usually means a desire to remain in one's own home. Yet, a person can age-in-place in a long-term care community, such as in assisted living. However, it is the responsibility of the aging loved one's caregiver(s) to help determine whether this preference is safe and appropriate and for how long.

AL: Assisted living. The preferred term is assisted living *community*, rather than facility. An assisted living community is private pay. It may be managed by a management company with corporate, family, private, or not-for-profit ownership. This distinction can make a difference in cost, staffing ratio, amenities, regulations, etc. An assisted living community is given certain regulations that determine the level of care that it can provide. This might mean that one AL can provide a higher level of care than another. For example, if a resident has a G-tube for feeding, that care need may not be able to be given by one AL, but can be by another AL. Each AL is different, although they may appear, at first glance, to be the same. Dementia care, often called by ALs "memory care," may or may not be provided or may depend on the person's stage, whether early stage, more advanced, or late stage.

An AL is not a nursing home. A widely held assumption is that ALs provide one-to-one care. They do not. I tell the families that I serve to look beyond the well-appointed presentation of the interior trappings and ask specifically about the level of care provided, exact information about transportation, the staff to resident ratio, the programs, amenities, and medical oversight options, and to get a clear understanding of how cost is structured. Also, an informed admissions person should be able to provide information about various ways to cover the cost.

Asset protection: This is an important issue to understand when faced with the need for long-term, custodial care. It is a strategy to preserve one's wealth to the extent possible, especially when there is the likelihood of needing care in a nursing home at some point in the care continuum. It is advisable to consult a certified financial planner and elder-law attorney to devise a financial plan that looks forward and backward.

Early in my career, I was approached by a woman's financial power of attorney. When I was contracted for consultation, the woman was about 101 years old. She had lived at an AL for many years, private paying the entire time. She had been financially secure her entire life and at ninety-six, she thought that she would not outlive her money. So, with full capacity, she instructed her POA to donate a substantial amount of money to a university. Unfortunately, she outlived her money. What she had left was her monthly income, which was not enough to cover the cost of AL, and she was not financially eligible for Medicaid because of the donation. The donation had to have been given less than five years before. Medicaid has a five-year look-back period. In other words, her donation would be a countable asset since the donation was made within the last five years. The woman's situation could have resulted in her being asked to leave because she could no longer afford to pay. In desperation, her POA asked me if it was possible for the university to return the donation. No. Unfortunately, neither the woman nor her POA had been guided by an asset protection plan.

Through my advocacy and collaboration with the AL, the AL was willing to accept her monthly income as payment due to her age and her tenure at the AL. As I understand it, an asset protection plan would have considered both her long-term care expenses and her desire to give away money, yet still cover her long-term care for as long as possible without her needing to apply for Medicaid, which would mean a move to a Medicaid-certified nursing home.

Dementia: The umbrella term for a variety of types of age-related diseases. Some researchers identify two dozen or more types of dementia, including the most common type, AD. But, there is vascular dementia, Lewy body dementia, frontotemporal dementia, and Parkinson's disease dementia, to name only a few. Dementia has stages, each with different manifestations. Stages are early onset to advanced.

During the coronavirus pandemic, I've been guiding a family, a couple with adult children who live thousands of miles away. In my initial consultation with the adult children, all that I was given was that their father was stubborn and hard of hearing, and that he was and had been the primary caregiver for their mother, who was very frail and did not speak. The adult children said that their father managed his meds, their mother's meds, and oversaw the household by buying groceries, driving, and so forth. When I asked how long it had been since either adult child had visited, they said it had been months, largely because of air travel restrictions due to the pandemic.

What I encountered was a highly intelligent man, their father, who is memory impaired; "mild dementia" was the geriatrician's stage noted. Regardless, day-to-day management of the household, care for the wife, and medications is now beyond his capacity. There is no such thing as having a "bit of dementia."

Discharge plan: A strategy for care that is developed in anticipation of discharge from a medical facility. The plan determines the level of care and likely the type of care that will be needed after the hospitalization. Be a strong advocate by insisting that planning begin early in the hospital stay. Also, appeal the discharge when necessary. There is an appeal process. The form should be given to you at admission. However, I have found that the form is rarely explained and is usually overlooked by family. Insist that a person's discharge can only be done when there is a safe and appropriate place to return to. If there is no one at home or no one to assist, even minimally, then a discharge and return home is neither safe nor appropriate. It is the hospital discharge planner's responsibility to determine a safe and appropriate discharge.

Thelma, now deceased, and her family fell victim to shoddy discharge planning. She was discharged home, alone, with complicated care needs. Little did the family member who picked her up from the hospital know that Thelma had complex care needs. It is my guess that because Thelma was well-spoken and crafty about her home situation, she convinced the hospital that returning home was possible. The hospital should have verified Thelma's home situation rather than listen to Thelma, who had no idea about what it took to manage meds, prepare the pureed food that she required, and take care of her sleeping and toileting needs in her two-story home. It is my guess that the hospital discharge planner needed to empty Thelma's bed, and so the path of least resistance was to listen to Thelma's explanation of her home care situation without verification.

I got an urgent call from Thelma's family the day after she was discharged. From the little information that I had from the family, I knew immediately that Thelma required a caregiver. In haste, with the help of one of my "go-to" home care agencies, I quickly found a caregiver and went along to Thelma's house, where I found her emaciated, alone, unsafe, and in distress. After getting urgent in-home one-to-one care in place, I immediately advocated for readmission. Thelma had a form of cancer that made it impossible for her to ingest food, ambulate, or care for herself.

I was able to get Thelma readmitted to the hospital. The care plan that I made included a discharge to a sub-acute and then admission to an AL, the length of stay to be determined based on her needs and financial situation. However, I knew from the outset that she could not return home and that her house would need to be sold to generate funds for her care. With the proceeds from the sale of her house, she was able to pay for care in an AL, where she thrived until her death.

Durable power of attorney (POA): A legal document that allows an individual to designate an "agent" to act on a person's behalf. A "durable" POA endures even if the individual becomes incapacitated. There are two kinds: financial and health.

In my practice, numerous times I find that a person has a POA but has not shared a copy with the person designated as their agent. Often I find that the agent or alternate agent is reluctant to act on the individual's behalf, even though the "power" and authority are there.

Almost without fail, I will encounter an adult child who is POA for a parent. At the assessment, I will ask whether there is a POA. Often, there is. The issue that I encounter is the reluctance of the agent to act.

Two instances come to mind. Mrs. Johnson (not her real name) has several adult children. When I asked about her POA, she shared a copy with me. On review, I noted that her older daughter was her agent and the younger daughter, the alternate. I knew the personality of each daughter. The older daughter was a creative type; the younger daughter, analytical, organized, and practical. I asked Mrs. Johnson why she appointed Karen (not her real name) as her agent. Mrs. Johnson said, "Because she's my oldest child." I then said to Mrs. Johnson, "Which one of your children has a head for details and follow-up?" Mrs. Johnson thought and answered, "Well, it's really Sandra (not her real name) and not Karen. I just picked Karen because she was older." I then said that she should consider Sandra as primary. She agreed and said that she only thought about designating her POA on the basis of age, not her daughters' attributes.

A reluctance to act on behalf of a parent when the time comes is something I encounter far too often with POAs. Granted, it is a tough role reversal for an adult child and their parent. I have an ongoing situation with a family as I pen these words. At this writing, I have been the family's geriatric care manager for about six months. The father designated a daughter as his financial POA. However, until my continued coaching, the daughter behaved with the father as if he had capacity. It took repeated consultation with the daughter to convince her that her father no longer had decision-making competency about key issues and that she needed to act on his behalf. Slowly, she's beginning to take the reins.

Accepting the role of someone's POA is a serious undertaking. Agree to the role only if you're willing to "step in" on the person's behalf.

Elder law attorney: An attorney who specializes in a wide range of legal issues related to aging. Elder law attorneys often collaborate with geriatric care managers to provide comprehensive consultation. Elder law attorneys are credentialed by the National Academy of Elder Law Attorneys (NAELA; www.NAELA.org).

A dear elderly man, Norman, had absolutely nothing in place in terms of legal documents when I started assisting him. Norman was financially secure and probably had a net worth of several million. He had a brother, somewhat estranged, and two nephews. Norman was divorced, but friendly with his former wife. Among my initial steps with Norman was to get him under the care of an elder law attorney. With the attorney, Norman did his POAs, established a trust, made a will, and did preneed funeral planning. At first, Norman proposed having me accompany him to a neighbor's law firm who had handled Norman's divorce. I had to educate him. I had a ready answer for Norman when he asked why he needed an elder law attorney, specifically: "Norman, if you had a heart issue, would you go to a cardiologist or would you go to a podiatrist?" Norman got the point.

Geriatrician; geriatrics; gerontology: A geriatrician is a medical doctor who specializes in the care of an older person. Geriatrics is the branch of medicine that deals with older people. Gerontology is the study of aging. Hence a gerontologist is an academic who has studied aging. An applied gerontologist is a person who puts into practice learnings derived from academic research and study.

Geriatricians are usually internists. A geriatrician becomes the primary care physician, or PCP. During a consultation, I asked a family member whether her loved one had had a hearing evaluation. She said, "I asked my father's internist about my father's hearing aids and his continued problems with his hearing." (This was before the family moved the father to a geriatrician.) "But I never got a response." I am confident that had her father been under the care of a geriatrician, the geriatrician would have referred the father to an otolaryngologist, an ear, nose, and throat doctor; and an audiologist, who fits and repairs hearing aids and administers hearing tests.

Another client, Pat, who is quite a character, repeatedly complained that she wasn't hearing too well. But under certain circumstances, Pat could hear quite well, especially when there was a bit of juicy gossip coming her way. I assumed that there was some degree of hearing loss—or so I thought. Off I took Pat to an ear, nose, and throat doctor. He took a look in her ears and saw that both ears were impacted with wax, called cerumen. When he removed the wax, Pat exclaimed, "Boy, I can hear much better!"

Health care directive: A written document that details a person's wishes and preferences about their health care. It allows a person to name someone to act on their behalf (an "agent") to carry out their wishes and preferences should they become unable to speak for themselves.

HIPAA: The Health Insurance Portability and Accountability Act, which mandates that a person's medical information be kept private and secure. Any person who requires any degree of care, regardless of age, can authorize another person or entity to receive, review, or have access to medical information. A health care POA can suffice to satisfy HIPAA. Or, a person can simply write out and sign a statement authorizing an individual to have access to medical information. Google "authorization to disclose health information" for the proper wording.

In my practice as a geriatric care manager, it is standard for me to require a simple written statement from each person that I serve that allows me to have access to their medical and health information. It is useful when there is no POA in place. Having such a written statement, I have found, eliminates impediments when I need information.

Hospice: A type of care that focuses on enhancing the quality of life, rather than extending life, for those with a terminal diagnosis. Hospice is a service, not a place. Hospice is one of the untapped benefits of Medicare insurance. Unfortunately, physicians and families continue to be reluctant to consider hospice because of prevailing myths and assumptions. Hospice care is delivered by a hospice company— private, corporate, or not-for-profit. For instance, in the Washington, DC, metro area there are approximately five companies that provide hospice. There are general criteria for a hospice-appropriate person, including dependence on help for three of six activities of daily living (ADLs) and an illness with a prognosis of approximately six months.

Chessley had been in and out of hospice care at the AL where he lived for three years. He was admitted and discharged from hospice because he continued to thrive. I had him tested recently for the COVID-19 virus. He tested positive, but was asymptomatic. Chessley had a hearty appetite, but had advanced dementia and required one-to-one private-pay care besides the care at AL. At first, three years ago, I had to convince his son that Chessley seemed to be hospice appropriate. The benefits were several: incontinence supplies, a Hoyer lift, and his medications were provided, along with the support of the hospice medical director, a visiting nurse, and an aide who visited Chessley for several hours each week.

Over the years, I'd been called at least three times to hear that Chessley seemed to be "actively dying." However, each time he rebounded and was discharged from hospice and later readmitted. This pattern of admission-discharge was somewhat unusual, and the length of hospice care was also unusual. Yet, it is possible.

Yesterday, I got a call from AL informing me that Chessley had died; I had guided his care for nearly four years. Hospice care afforded him the chance to die on his terms.

IL: Independent living. A useful way to think about IL is "freedom from daily household tasks and chores." Several of the people I have served, particularly women, move to IL because they are tired of cooking, cleaning, and doing laundry! At the IL level, a person is safely able to complete ADLs independently or with some assistance. Whether a person is at an IL level in AL depends on an assessment.

Levels of care: A system to designate the degree of medical care or supportive care that a person requires. Each level corresponds to the complexity of care needed.

Vivian (not her real name) moved into a senior care community to be near her daughter. Vivian's husband had died only a few months before she moved to the senior care community. Vivian presented as clinically depressed; her daughter reported that her mother spent long hours "in bed." Her daughter also reported that her mother wasn't particularly sociable and tended to "keep to herself."

During the first weeks of Vivian's new residence, her daughter was concerned. She felt that her mother didn't fit in because some residents there were in wheelchairs. Vivian was assessed at level 1. In this community, that level provided for meals, a room, programs, laundry, and so on. Vivian's medication management was an add-on expense.

With prompts and support, Vivian has become active, highly sociable, and goes out and about on her own—she has flourished. Within a senior care community that provides levels of care from IL to Memory, to date, Vivian remains at IL.

Living will: A document detailing a person's desires regarding their medical treatment in circumstances in which they are no longer able to express informed consent. In my work, I recommend that each family member in addition to the aging loved one complete "Five Wishes" (see www.fivewishes.org). "Five Wishes" is a document recognized in all but a few states. The document makes known an individual's preferences and wishes in the event that they are unable to make their own decisions.

I have had my own family complete "Five Wishes." Should I become unable to groom myself on my own, one wish of mine is for someone to make sure that my lip and chin are hair-free. I even share this "wish" in presentations that I give. People really laugh when I share this particular "wish." Call it vanity or not, but I would welcome visitors should I become ill or incapacitated in some way, and I prefer that no one who might come to visit me encounter a "wolf woman"!

While this has become a joke among family and friends, my son assures me not to worry, that he will always be sure that he will never have a wolf mom!

My point is to illustrate that "Five Wishes" or another form of living will can be as specific and detailed as a person wants it to be.

Look-back period: To qualify for Medicaid, a person has to be asset and medically eligible. Total assets cannot exceed a certain amount, which varies from state to state. The asset limit is usually under $3,000. To apply for Medicaid, any money given away within five years of the date a person applies for Medicaid would be considered an asset and counted as such for Medicaid eligibility. Any money or transfer made prior to five years (the look-back period) is outside the purview of Medicaid and, therefore, not counted as an asset.

Spend-down: This refers to any direct expense for a person to "spend down" assets to meet Medicaid eligibility. In other words, Medicaid requires that a person be impoverished, first, in order to qualify. Medicaid is not a free ride, as many people think.

Ma Nichols, as she was lovingly called by the assisted living community where she resided for nearly five years, was a typical situation. Ma Nichols's house was sold. With the proceeds from the sale of her home, her monthly income, and some financial support from her family, Ma Nichols was able to private pay at a senior care community for four and a half years. (The average cost of that community was about $13,000 per month.)

When Ma Nichols had depleted and spent down to just over $2,000, she was able to qualify for Medicaid and move to a Medicaid-certified community, since she could no longer pay for private care.

In caring for an aging loved one, attention must be given to an overall financial plan for long-term care. For the average family, understanding the "spend-down" process is key to informed eldercare.

LTC or long-term care: This phrase means that a person will require what is known as custodial care for an extended period of time. Long-term care can be provided at home or in a senior living community, whether IL, AL, or a nursing home.

MCD: This is the abbreviation for mild cognitive decline, also called mild cognitive impairment or MCI. MCD or MCI means that a person may have short-term memory problems, executive functioning challenges (such as managing finances), or times of getting lost or sundowning (late-day confusion or irritability). MCD or MCI may be an early stage dementia.

John (not his real name) was recently diagnosed with MCD by a new doctor, a geriatrician. Yet according to his family, his former doctor, an internist, never gave John any diagnosis. John is high functioning and has devised creative ways to compensate for his MCD. As is often the case, his family was slow to recognize the extent of his impairment. Recently, John asked his family for a substantial amount of cash. His family gave him the money. The family reasoned that they gave it to him because he asked for it and it was John's money, not theirs.

A senior-serving professional would have immediately recognized that John's capacity to manage a substantial amount of cash was no longer possible. However, his family was still facing the difficult work of adjusting to John's cognitive decline.

Medicaid vs. Medicare: These are two different programs. Medicaid is a public assistance program based on financial and medical need and paid for by each state's collected taxes. Medicaid covers long-term care, but is usually restricted to care in a nursing home. Medicare is a health insurance provided to people over sixty-five. There are two main parts to Medicare: part A for inpatient, hospital services and part B for outpatient medical services, such as doctor's visits, rehab services, and so on.

Medication management: This aspect of senior care is too often overlooked. Medication mistakes are frequent and can lead to unintended consequences. Eldercare-givers must pay close attention to how a loved one's medications are dispensed, managed, and administered. I advise eldercare-givers to think about "the taking of pills" as a highly complex process. It is a process that requires a system, monitoring, and oversight, especially when there is any degree of MCI. It can be worth it to pay a professional to manage medications for a loved one with complete oversight and coordination with the senior's doctors.

One incident readily comes to mind. Evelyn was in a Medicare advantage program which covered her medications. However, that pharmacy did not deliver. So, I would pick up Evelyn's prescriptions. Evelyn was sharp as a tack but she had low vision. I checked the medicine bottles before leaving the pharmacy. One time, I was given the wrong person's prescriptions because she had a similar name! I doubt, even with a delivery, that Evelyn with her low vision would have been able to read pill bottle labels. And likely, she would not have checked her name. This pharmacy mistake led to my getting Evelyn a magnifier with specific steps to follow when a prescription was delivered: that is, check the name, check the dosage, check the name of the medication, check the color, and so on.

I had a similar experience with May (not her real name). May is legally blind. But she is able to compensate, to some degree, with visual aids. With my guidance, May moved from her home where she lived alone to an AL. There she insisted that she could manage her medications. She felt that she could save money by not having to pay for medication management. The family signed a waiver for her to do this since she had been managing her medications at home. (Yet, her family never witnessed how well and if she was truly able to do so. They simply went on what she told them.) When I found out that May was self-medicating, I contacted the AL's executive director. No question, May was at risk and she would have to have her medications managed and administered by the AL community.

Medicare appeal process: Upon admission to the hospital, each patient is given a form, "How to Appeal a Medicare Decision." I've never encountered any person or their family who actually reads or understands what the form is about and for. Take note. If it seems that a discharge is not safe or appropriate, there is a way to appeal. It only requires a phone call to start the process. A hospital cannot discharge a patient when an appeal is in progress. This is an important form for eldercare providers to know about.

Geriatric care managers are often called in during the middle of a crisis. Very often, the crisis involves a discharge. I remember the Aldens (not their real name). The father was about to be discharged, but he lived alone. Both of his children lived out of town. I remember the scramble of trying to determine a last-minute discharge plan. The hospital social worker said that no beds were available in a sub-acute for this patient. I wondered why and requested to read his chart. Prior to this, I told the family to appeal the discharge while I tried to discover what was what.

I reviewed his chart and was shocked at one note: "pt (patient) spreads feces on walls. . . ." There was absolutely no behavior like this that Mr. Alden had ever displayed. I set about demanding an explanation. It turned out that Mr. Alden had been turned away by countless sub-acutes because he was stigmatized as having "difficult behavior," which was a "mischart."

There are many reasons to start an appeal. Whatever the reason, it is an avenue to pursue if the discharge is unsafe or inappropriate. Use those words and be able to say why.

Observation status vs. admission: People who need to be monitored for any reason may be assigned to a hospital bed, but be on "observation status," which does not constitute an admission. There are other reasons to put a person on "observation status," driven by insurance and reimbursement. To be eligible for admission to a sub-acute, a patient must be on observation status for at least three days. Always ask to determine a person's hospital status because there are different implications for each.

Nola relied on me as a daughter. Her own daughter predeceased her. Her attentive son was always responsive, but there were certain things that she felt comfortable asking me to do, not her son. Once, she needed to buy new underwear. She was a cancer survivor for many years. She needed mastectomy bras and asked me to take her to be fitted. Off we went to the corset shop; her son drove us there. Nola and I became very close.

Nola had progressive supranuclear palsy (PSP), a rare and debilitating disease. Eventually, she lost her speech, so she always had to be accompanied during a hospital stay. Explanation was always needed . . . she was not living with dementia, but with PSP, with no cognitive impairment. During Nola's last hospitalization, she was in excruciating pain from a broken arm. The pain was difficult to control. I remember this unusual situation clearly. I wanted to know whether Nola was on observation status or whether she had been admitted. At this point she had been in the hospital several days. No one could provide an answer. As it turned out, for reasons I will never understand, Nola remained on observation status for well over a week before being discharged. She was never actually admitted.

Personal care agreement: Also known as a personal service contract, this is a document outlining the care that a person, usually a family member, will provide in exchange for financial compensation. Google "personal care agreement" for samples.

POD (payable on death): This is a banking arrangement that can be designated on a person's bank accounts. Different from a "joint account," this arrangement designates a beneficiary to receive the assets in the accounts upon the account holder's death.

An incident from my own caregiving with my father: the standard, we thought, was for my father and me to have a joint account as his account. This, of course, allowed me to have access to his money. But, that joint ownership only allowed me to have access during his lifetime. Soon after he died, I needed to pay caregivers and wrote checks on the "joint" account. However, the money in the account was my father's money; that is the distinction. Although it was a joint account, the account was funded by my father's money. What happened next was a fiasco. The direct deposit from social security and another direct deposit were reversed since he died a day or so before the direct deposits hit his account. So, checks to pay caregivers bounced. Ugh! Next, somehow the bank withdrew the overdraft from *my* account, presumably because as a joint owner, I had to give the bank my social security number. No one had even suggested that it would have been far better had my father's accounts been set up as POD accounts. Lesson learned. Lesson passed on to other eldercare-givers.

Respite stay: A short-term stay in a senior care community, often following a hospitalization and before a return home. It can also be a period to give family a break from caregiving. Respite stays are private pay or covered by a long-term care insurance benefit. One corporate-owned assisted living community recently promoted a respite program called "The Road Home," a thirty-day respite stay. Some communities will extend a respite stay. Ask.

SNF: Skilled nursing facility. A facility that provides the highest level of care.

Sub-acute care: Complex or rehabilitative care provided by a nursing facility, rather than in a hospital or rehab facility.

Trust (revocable; irrevocable): A property interest held by one person or organization (such as a bank) for the benefit of another. A revocable trust can be broken, while an irrevocable trust cannot. Often used to preserve assets for ongoing care expenses or for future generations, trusts are complicated and require sound financial and legal advice to set up.

Will: A legal document outlining one's wishes for distribution of one's assets after death.

Skills to Practice and Master

One skill to master is "therapeutic fibbing." While controversial for some practitioners, I've found it useful to think of this skill as "artful omission." Regardless, the goal is to avoid conflict and lessen anxiety for the caregiver and care recipient.

> **Care receiver:** "When are you going on vacation? Where are you going? How long will you be away?"

> **Caregiver:** "I haven't worked through all the details yet, because I checked at work and I didn't get an answer about my vacation. Another co-worker is out on extended sick leave."

I've coached many caregivers to find a way around questions that may confuse or cause anxiety for an aging loved one. As my father's caregiver and his only child, any time I gave my father specific answers, it only caused him distress. I was his primary point of contact. If something were to happen to me, what would he do? Soon after college, my son—my father's only grandchild—traveled internationally as a professional musician. At first, my son would excitedly share his upcoming gigs, in the States or elsewhere. We soon realized that sharing his various gigs caused my father too much anxiety. So we had to find ways around his questions and refrain from giving him "too much information."

I did lots of coaching for Dennis, a former client. Dennis was his mother's only surviving child and his son was her only grandchild. Dennis and his family took yearly summer vacations. Dennis's mother's life had been filled with losses—her husband, daughter, aunts, and mother had all passed away, and her father had been killed suspiciously when she was young. Dennis's mother was a resident in an assisted living community. The vacation that was planned during his mother's first year in assisted living was a weeklong stay, miles away. Dennis understandably wanted to share the details of the upcoming vacation trip. I suggested that it might not be the wisest thing to do. At first, Dennis felt that not telling his mother would be dishonest. I coached Dennis about giving too much information and I shared how my father would become too anxious when he knew that I or Guillermo would be out of reach and "away."

Unfortunately, the literature is full of vignettes by family caregivers who are sabotaged by their loved one when there were plans for the caregiver to be "away." The person receiving care gets sick, falls, or creates some reason that "requires" the family caregiver not to leave. Slowly, Dennis came to accept that it wasn't helpful to give information that would be anxiety-producing. It took him several tries to gain the skill of "artful omission," the judicious use of therapeutic "fiblets." "Do no harm, but share little," is what I say to family caregivers.

Validation Therapy

Validation therapy, in the world of caregiving, simply means to validate the care receiver's reality and, in doing so, turn the care receiver's attention elsewhere.

> **Care receiver:** "You didn't tell me about a doctor's appointment or else I would remember. There's nothing wrong with my memory!"
>
> **Caregiver:** "I'm sorry. I forgot to tell you."
>
> (Don't respond by saying, "You've been seeing the doctor every three months for the last two years. And plus,

it's written on your calendar. I told you about it yesterday and this morning.")

Here's another example, particularly applicable for a caregiver for someone who is cognitively impaired.

Care receiver: "Yesterday, I talked to my mother; she visited me."

Caregiver: "Tell me about the visit. What did you talk about?"

(Don't say, "That's impossible, what are you talking about? Your mother is dead.")

Recently, I had to remind Margaret, a seasoned professional caregiver (not her real name), about this important skill. Margaret complained to me that she simply would not continue caring for June. Each time she would arrive to start care, June would tell Margaret to leave; she wasn't needed because June's daughter would come over to help her. Margaret became increasingly frustrated and called me to complain that June didn't appreciate her. On one occasion, Margaret called June's daughter in front of June, trying to prove to June that she, not the daughter, was there to help June.

Margaret forgot the second important skill. Rather than trying to prove something to June, Margaret could have tried to console June by redirecting her attention to how lovely the day was or some other such distraction. Margaret needed to remember that the goal was not to prove herself right and June wrong, but rather to make June feel content and secure.

Limit Choices and Problem-Solve

I didn't realize how much of a daddy's girl I was until I became my father's family caregiver. I remember when it dawned on me. My father had specific preferences about his food, his clothes, and his appearance, as we all do. One Sunday morning I left my house and went to pick up my father for church. He wasn't ready to leave. His caregiver asked me to come in. I found my father stumped about which tie to wear. I began to sort through various colors and patterns with him, trying to get him to decide on a tie. Enrique, my husband, asked why it had taken so long for me to pick up my father. I recounted the tie selection process.

He asked, "Irene, about how long did you and your father go through that exercise?" His question made me think. I had spent one whole hour on this very minor matter. I realized that to be an effective caregiver I needed to limit choices. It is one of the important lessons I share with caregivers, regardless of the care receiver's age.

Recognize Your Limits

Determine what you can and cannot do. If changing a soiled disposable product is something that you simply can't stomach, problem-solve and find a way around the challenge.

Enrique reminds me that when our son Guillermo was born, I gagged the first time I had to change his diaper. Fast-forward to years later, when I had to care for my father. Early on, before I realized how I struggled in this area, I tried to ignore my reaction to the smells and odors that can accompany an illness. Frankly, I was ashamed. Finally, I figured out that if I used a mask to cover my nose and mouth, I could handle assisting with toileting. Eventually, I learned to joke about it and do what had to be done.

Manipulation Masters

Be aware of manipulation and sabotage. My father was a consummate manipulator until I caught on. I remember one time very clearly. Before I entered my father's apartment, where he was cared for by a live-in caregiver, I heard loud laughing, my father's, through the door. I knocked and entered. I found my father slumped over in his wheelchair. But he was clearly alive. Many times, my father tried all kinds of ways to invite me to the pity-poo parties that he sometimes held for himself! I refused to attend. Be on the lookout for possible manipulation by a loved one you're caring for.

Resist Ignoring Aberrant Behaviors

We must acknowledge certain symptoms and become attuned to seeing and accepting the signs of cognitive and physical changes or decline.

Ernest's father, who was in his mid-eighties, lived alone in a two-bedroom condo. Ernest lived five hours away. His work was such that regular visits were impossible. However, after one visit with his father, Ernest called me to say he didn't think all was well with his father and he needed my help. When I met with his father, I could tell all wasn't well. His personal care was compromised. There was spoiled food in the refrigerator and piles of newspapers and mail littered all over the room. A stench permeated his home. There were signs galore that likely signaled to Ernest that all wasn't well. However, he failed to recognize the extent of his father's condition. Likely, Ernest had resorted to denial in order not to become overwhelmed. However, denial, while a coping mechanism, is ill-serving when it comes to eldercare.

Some Other Helpful Tips

1. Stop asking for permission from the care receiver.

2. Use a homecare agency to hire a professional caregiver, or if a caregiver is contracted directly, pay the required taxes. Regardless, determine the scope of work.

3. Make sure all estate documents are in place—yours and the care receiver's.

4. Avoid having to say, "I promised my dad that I would never put him in a nursing home." Never, never make promises that may be impossible to keep.

5. Use a senior-serving professional; don't go it alone. Below are several to know about and keep in your elder-care toolbox. You should also find out what services and advice are available, often for free, from your local Agency on Aging.

   Aging Life Care Association (formerly National Association of Professional Geriatric Care Managers)
   www.aginglifecare.org

   American Association of Daily Money Managers
   www.secure.aadmm.com

   Society of Certified Senior Advisors
   www.csa.us

   National Academy of Elder Law Attorneys
   www.naela.org

   National Association of Senior Move Managers
   www.nasmm.org

CHAPTER EIGHT

Three Books on Compassion and Care

Anyone involved in eldercare has little time left to read, given the demands of eldercare in whatever form it takes. So, here I will offer an overview of three books. These are useful resources to help a caregiver to "tool up": *Being Mortal: Medicine and What Matters in the End* by Atul Gawande[1]; *Staring at the Sun: Overcoming the Terror of Death* by Irvin D. Yalom[2]; and *The Age of Dignity: Preparing for the Elder Boom in a Changing America* by Ai-Jen Poo with Ariane Conrad.[3] Two authors are medical doctors, two have received MacArthur Awards, and all three provide provocative and insightful explorations of aging through personal experiences, clinical illustrations, and

---

1. Atul Gawande, *Being Mortal: Medicine and What Matters in the End* (New York: Henry Holt and Co., 2014).

2. Irvin D. Yalom, *Staring at the Sun: Overcoming the Terror of Death* (San Francisco: Jossey-Bass, 2008).

3. Ai-Jen Poo with Ariane Conrad, *The Age of Dignity: Preparing for the Elder Boom in a Changing America* (New York: New Press, 2015).

research. Each book can stand on its own, but they share several common themes:

- death is the natural order of things;
- sooner or later *independence* becomes impossible due to illness or infirmity;
- eldercare needs to be reinvented—from a medically dominated enterprise to an eldercare culture that enables well-being;
- care is the most powerful expression of our human interconnectedness and interdependence;
- care is essential to every living being;
- when there's no *cure*, there's usually the need for *care*;
- surgical/medical interventions and maintenance often cannot deliver what we want—they often only prolong the crumbling of one's bodily systems;
- "death anxiety" is at the heart of much anxiety, expressed in a wellspring of symptoms, worries, stresses, and conflicts;
- the longer one lives, the more likely one will need some form of assistance/care.

Each author offers personal vignettes, clinical illustrations, and advocacy efforts; each book notes the centrality of caregiving in the life of the individual who faces illness, death, infirmity, isolation, trauma, loss, and the many other challenges that accompany aging. All three speak to the need for a reframing of our commonly held notions about caregivers and caregiving.

First, let's make a distinction between *caregiving* and *caretaking*; the words are used interchangeably, but there is a difference. A *caretaker* takes care of a building or land, such as a caretaker for a cemetery or garden. A *caregiver* helps, protects, and supports a person. Caregiving is all-encompassing. It can include helping in all its manifestations: aid, safety, protection from harm. Each author shares stories from their own family, from patients, and from informants; in each story, the author is caregiving as a caregiver.

In *The Age of Dignity*, Poo celebrates Mrs. Sun, her grandmother's family caregiver, as indispensable to the family. Poo honed her own caregiving skills as she learned about what it meant to be a family member with an aging loved one. She is a fierce advocate for in-home caregivers. She laments the low wages earned by professional caregivers and the "dishonor" often accorded them. Poo is an activist and advocate: the "caregiver's caregiver." She cofounded Domestic Workers United, the New York organization that spearheaded the Domestic Workers' Bill of Rights in 2010 that called for better wages, improved working conditions, insurance, and other quality-of-life issues absent from the lives of most professional caregivers.

Poo's advocacy centers on what she calls a "Care Grid." The Care Grid she envisions "brings together public, private, and nonprofit resources and creates a comprehensive, coordinated system in which elders can age with dignity and their caregivers, both professional paid workers and unpaid family or friends, can thrive as well."[4] She goes on to examine "secure social security," "home care for all," twenty-first-century care jobs, and "a caregiving citizenship." We all recognize, hopefully, that such a Care Grid needs to be in place now.

In *Staring at the Sun*, psychiatrist Irvin Yalom—a "professional caregiver"—provides clinical illustrations about

---

4. Poo with Conrad, *Age of Dignity*, 155.

death and how he cared for his patients to help them deal with what he calls "death anxiety." A reader's guide included at the end of the book contains what are essentially study questions, useful to a caregiver when faced with care for someone who has spoken or unspoken "death anxiety." I have excerpted some of the questions that I think are useful for reflection.

- Do you agree that confronting death is like staring into the sun—something painful, difficult, but necessary if we are to go on living as fully conscious individuals?[5]

- Much of our anxiety and psychopathology can be traced back to death anxiety. Do you agree?[6]

- What is your greatest fear associated with death?[7]

- Have you ever had an "awakening experience" in your life, a major illness, divorce, loss of a job, retirement, death of a loved one, powerful dream, or significant reunion?[8]

Yalom's clinical illustration about Alice, a patient, is instructive. As a caregiver, are you empathetic and skilled enough to understand the experience of a paralyzing panic? Alice was distressed because she had to sell her home and its collection of musical instruments: "I can't sit still . . . I'm so edgy, I feel I'm going to burst." Yalom probed with questions and she answered, "[T]he pain is too raw. This is death surrounding me. Death everywhere. I want to scream." He guided Alice toward the "root" of

5. Yalom, *Staring at the Sun*, 294.
6. Yalom, *Staring at the Sun*, 293.
7. Yalom, *Staring at the Sun*, 295.
8. Yalom, *Staring at the Sun*, 295.

her anguish: "I just don't want to leave this life," she said. His explanations and analysis do nothing to calm her fears. Yalom writes, "I held her, stayed with her." He then gives a succinct instruction: "Hold the suffering one in any way that gives comfort." He goes on to add, "Sheer presence is the greatest gift you can offer anyone facing death (or a physically healthy person in a death panic)."[9]

Atul Gawande's *Being Mortal: Medicine and What Matters in the End* is a masterful, footnote-dense compilation about aging, living abundantly with dignity, death, and the medical profession's incompetence in handling these realities of life. The book has been an international best seller. As such, it attests to the nearly universal complexity of how "developed" societies struggle with medical interventions in the face of chronic illness, end-of-life care, and death. We must note that many non-Western cultures with traditional practices about aging and death are without the anxieties that surround aging and death, which is to state something quite obvious: "death anxiety" may well be a phenomenon of the West. In many non-Western societies, the elderly are revered, honored, and cared for, and death is a joining, or a return to "the elders," rather than "the end."

Gawande writes, "This is a book about the modern experience of mortality—about what it's like to be creatures who age and die, how medicine has changed the experience [of aging and death] and how it hasn't, where our ideas about how to deal with our finitude have got the reality wrong."[10]

He shares his personal experience of being the caregiver for his own parents, who were also physicians. He tells about his own inadequacy and that of his mother's in grap-

---

9. Yalom, *Staring at the Sun*, 130.
10. Gawande, *Being Mortal*, 9.

pling with his father's and her husband's decline in health and eventual death. Gawande writes that he learned a lot of things in medical school, but "mortality wasn't one of them."[11] His writing is both clinical and informational. The reader moves among vignettes about his patients to historical information about institutional care, starting from the 1950s and the beginning of nursing homes, to the 1980s when the "living center with assistance" concept (now known as assisted living) was formulated, to the 1990s and the emergence of corporate-owned, private-pay, senior housing: assisted living, retirement communities, senior housing, naturally occurring retirement communities, and continuing care retirement communities (CCRCs), or life care communities.

Gawande shares one incident as a caregiver for his father: "I helped him to the bathroom and swiveled him onto the seat," Gawande—doctor, professional caregiver, family caregiver—writes. Eventually he had to insert a catheter in his father to relieve the urine that would not come. "It's not something a person ever thinks they will come to. He had his eyes shut the entire time."[12]

As I was doing my final edits for this book, the coronavirus struck. For the last months, and likely into the foreseeable future, many more of us will become eldercare-givers. Seniors who have a compromised immune system and comorbidities are especially vulnerable to the virus. As a result of the pandemic, whether on the frontline of care or not, few will avoid providing some degree of care for a senior, whether grocery shopping or simply a telephone call. We're all touched by eldercare.

11. Gawande, *Being Mortal*, 1.
12. Gawande, *Being Mortal*, 254.

CHAPTER NINE

The High Cost of Eldercare

As I write, we are facing another presidential election. With the coronavirus pandemic that disproportionally strikes older people and people in long-term care facilities, the older population is finally on everyone's radar. What will be done to address the health issues for the ten thousand Americans who turn sixty-five each day? What happens to the three hundred thousand Americans who turn sixty-five each month and the 3.6 million Americans who will reach sixty-five each year? According to the Pew Research Center, this trend will continue full tilt until 2030.[1]

The cost of care, particularly long-term or custodial care, wherever it is delivered—in the home, in a senior living community, or in an institutional setting, such as a nursing home—is way beyond the financial grasp of most. Unfortunately, many people still believe that Medicare

---

1. D'Vera Cohn and Paul Taylor, "Baby Boomers Approach 65—Glumly," Pew Research Center: Social & Demographic Trends, December 20, 2010, https://www.pewsocialtrends.org/2010/12/20/baby-boomers-approach-65-glumly/.

covers the cost of custodial care. It does not. For the most part, Medicaid covers care in an institutional setting such as a nursing home. To date, state funding of the public program called Money Follows the Person (MFP) is limited, with long waiting lists for acceptance. MFP focuses on relocating Medicaid beneficiaries from institutions to community settings.

Dennis, his mother Nola's only child, struggled to make a decision to relocate his mother. Dennis contacted me years before he got to his "wit's end." After several conversations with me over several years, Dennis realized his long-distance caregiving for his mother was not sustainable or safe. He had to contend with his mother's daily barrage of telephone calls, calls from caregivers because his mother refused to let them in the house, and the homecare agency's calls because the caregivers called the agency about Nola's lack of cooperation for care. Dennis's mother lived in her own home, which was a twelve-hour drive from him. Dennis was a member of the sandwich generation: wedged between his wife and son and his mother. Plus, he had a robust professional life. With assistance from me, he was able to accept that the time was right for a move. With a range of care coordination, Nola was relocated and settled into a senior community, minutes from Dennis's house. As the relocation was being planned, I told Dennis to do the math to determine the cost for his mother's care. I told him to consider $10,000+ per month.

"What?" Dennis exclaimed. "How could that be?"

He was a financial professional, but could not understand why the projected cost of his mother's care as determined in the relocation care plan so far exceeded the cost of care cited in the Genworth Cost of Care survey.[2] This online resource offered by a long-term care insurance company is an excellent starting point for comparing the cost of long-term care (with a professional caregiver), a homemaker, an assisted living community, or a skilled nursing home. The survey cites and compares data for individual states. However, the survey does not consider the add-ons or hidden costs of long-term care, such as level of care, medications, supplies, and transportation, that can greatly add to the overall cost.

Even those fortunate enough to have long-term care insurance realize that the monthly benefit rarely covers the full cost of care wherever it is delivered. At the present time, I have two clients, both women in their mid-seventies, each with a monthly long-term care benefit of $10,000 per month. One continues to live at home (with professional caregivers) and the other lives in an assisted living community. On average, the cost for each one exceeds their long-term care benefit by thousands of dollars. Unimaginable, but unfortunately true.

Several years ago, my friend Linda, who lives outside the United States, called in desperation. Linda and I are childhood friends and our fathers were friends from their high school days. At the time she called, her father was in his mid-nineties. Linda's mother had died years before. Linda's father followed the usual trajectory of care arrangements: home with no help, home with a homemaker, home with an aide, short-term care in rehab after a hospitalization, and finally an eight-person "board and care home" where he died at one hundred and two. Linda's father had a long-

---

2. https://www.genworth.com/aging-and-you/finances/cost-of-care .html

term care insurance (LTCI) policy, but it had been over-looked until I urged the family to do some digging and find it. The policy, purchased years before, only covered care in a nursing home. Therefore, Linda's father had to pay out of pocket for his stay in the small assisted living home where he died. (Newer long-term care policies are not as restrictive as older ones like the one Linda's father had. Nowadays, most long-term care policies follow the individual, rather than being restricted to a particular setting.)

Linda's misunderstanding of long-term care and Dennis's sticker shock are all too common. Linda assumed that long-term care referred to care in a facility, exclusively. She didn't realize that long-term care simply meant that care would be needed for the rest of the person's life. And Dennis did not realize that the Genworth survey did not include the hidden and full costs of long-term care. The National Care Planning Council's website (www.longterm carelink.net) is an extensive resource for understanding and planning for long-term care.

Consider this: the concept of insurance for an automobile only became mandatory in 1927. My father would have been fourteen years old. While his father was a property owner in Washington, DC, and was a federal employee, it is doubtful that the family owned an automobile. In fact, the family lore is that my father was the first in his family to own a car—and he was probably in his twenties. For people in my father's generation, the concept of car insurance was something new. Similarly, in that generation, long-term care insurance was not understood and not readily acquired.

My friend Marsha, when she worked for a major corporation, tried to encourage her parents to take advantage of the long-term care group plan that her employer offered.

Marsha was corporate counsel for the corporation and was well aware of the protection and value of getting a long-term care insurance policy. But try as she did, her parents would not budge. My mother was a planner and was very attentive to aging issues and health coverage because of her chronic health challenges. But neither she, nor my father, had the foresight to obtain a long-term care insurance policy. It was a concept outside of my parent's generation, just like it was for Marsha's parents, who were of the same generation as my parents.

It is likely that my parents and others in their cohort decided not to take out a long-term care policy because the care benefit only covered care in a "nursing home"—considered then, and often now, as a dreaded place to live. Recall Linda's father's early policy; he was in the same age cohort as Marsha's and my parents.

In early times, families cared for their loved ones at home. Many people now in their eighties and older continue to regard the nursing home as an iteration of the poorhouse, almshouse, sanitarium, or rest home—all places to be avoided. Nursing homes only came into existence in the 1960s along with long-term care insurance. I encounter families who are held hostage as they try to accommodate an aging loved one at home, struggling to live out a promise to "Never, never put me in a nursing home, never!" The nursing home is often considered a place of dread, horror, disgrace, and loneliness to be avoided at any cost. Unfortunately, in many situations, that is the case.

As a result, seniors over eighty (and their adult children) often associate long-term care exclusively with care in a *nursing home*. A large part of my work has been to educate and inform families to help them navigate the range of care options. I've come up with a pithy definition for caregivers to broaden their understanding of what long-term care means: custodial care that a person requires from someone else to help them with physical and emotional needs over an extended period of time. I stress that long-term care can be delivered in a variety of settings.

Navigating Murky Water

The murky water of long-term care options has no standard nomenclature. Even within the same city, there can be a variety of names for places that provide eldercare. Facility #1 calls itself an "assisted living community," but does not provide long-term care for people living with memory impairment or living on a ventilator, for example. Facility #2 calls itself an "active senior community," but also offers several levels of care from independent to nursing care, depending on the resident's care needs. Facility #3 calls itself a "small assisted living home," but provides only room and board without a high level of care. Even an informed consumer isn't prepared for the array of formats, care provisions, and options.

I already noted in chapter 7 that, as more than a matter of semantics, the preferred way is to refrain from calling any long-term care community a "facility." The word depersonalizes the setting. Rather, use "assisted living community," "long-term care community," or "senior residence." And the people needing care in these communities are *residents*, not patients.

In my practice, I have gotten too many panicky calls to count from families when a loved one is about to be discharged from the hospital. The discharge summary has clear instructions: "Your loved one will need 24/7 care." Panic ensues. The options and costs are staggering.

Long-term or custodial care is, often, assistance with some or all the basic tasks of life, the activities of daily living (ADLs)—dressing, personal care, and so on. Long-term care can also be assistance with *instrumental* activities of daily living (IADLs)—managing money, managing medications, shopping, scheduling appointments, transportation, and household maintenance, for example.

What a Family Caregiver Needs to Know

Besides the direct cost of long-term care wherever it is provided, there are a host of other expenses that are often overlooked or even not anticipated. For example, many senior-care communities tell prospective residents that transportation to and from appointments is provided. Ask follow-up questions: Is there an additional cost for this service? Is it available only to certain locations or on certain days of the week? How much notice is required to arrange transportation? I advise clients to look beyond the glitter, smiling faces, and fine dining when considering long-term care for a loved one in a senior community. What about caregiver training and the ratio of caregivers to residents?

It is a challenge to navigate the murky water of long-term care no matter where it is delivered. Far too often, families confront the cost of care—with little assistance or planning—when they have to take the plunge into murky water after a loved one's hospital stay, which means they are reactive as they try to make a decision in the middle of a crisis. Misunderstanding and lack of information abound. When considering a move to an assisted living community, it is important to understand that it is real estate: a space, a building, room and board. Care is provided at an additional cost. A few situations offer a bundled cost that includes room and board, meals, programs, and care level, but this format seems to be limited nationwide. Accept that even in an assisted living setting, a caregiving role for the family or friend of the loved one will still be required.

The *Los Angeles Times* published an article in 2002, "Assisted Living's Hidden Fees." It cited a 1999 report by the General Accounting Office, the investigative arm of Congress, that stated:

> Marketing material, contracts, and other written material provided by the facilities [long-term care facilities] are often incomplete and are sometimes vague or misleading [and] only 25% of facilities routinely provide their document to prospective residents before they decide to apply for admission.[3]

Though that article was published years ago, much remains the same. As mentioned in chapter 7, more recently an article published in the *New York Times* pointed out that high cost doesn't translate into good resident care.[4]

The Consumer Consortium on Assisted Living developed a guidebook with Metropolitan Life Insurance. The guide is only available through MetLife or a financial advisory firm such as Wells Fargo Advisors. The booklet includes questions for families to ask when considering a long-term care facility. Most of the questions posed have an answer that involves a cost. Long-term care is expensive,

---

3. Bob Rosenblatt, "Assisted Living's Hidden Fees," *Los Angeles Times*, July 22, 2002, https://www.latimes.com/archives/la-xpm-2002 -jul-22-he-bob22-story.html.

4. Paula San, "Some Assisted-Living Residents Don't Get Promised Care, Suit Charges," *New York Times*, February 14, 2020, https://www .nytimes.com/2020/02/14/health/assisted-living-staffing.html.

and the cost of care wherever it is given rises about 4 percent annually. Following is a more in-depth overview of some of the hidden or overlooked costs that can come with long-term, custodial care.

Transportation

It will not always be safe, convenient, or possible to transport your older loved one in a car. Public transportation—even if it is accessible—is often unreliable and is even more unsafe. Private wheelchair accessible transportation comes with a cost. Just recently, a client needed transportation for his mother to attend his father's funeral. It would not have been safe or comfortable to get her in and out of a car. They needed a wheelchair van, but that cost $200. If they had not rented the van, his mother would not have been able to attend her husband's funeral.

My father became paralyzed and then a double amputee, which meant he required wheelchair transportation after his ability to transfer from his wheelchair to the car became physically taxing for him, for me, and for his professional male caregiver. As his family caregiver, figuring out how to get him out of the house became a major undertaking for me, even with a code-compliant ramp. Once, I was maneuvering him out of his lift-equipped wheelchair van and both of us nearly slid out because the lift wasn't level. I am grateful for a passerby who caught my father by his collar before his head hit the sidewalk! Thinking back on that day still makes me cringe. Keep in mind that there may come a time when a personal care assistant or a certified nursing assistant, is necessary, or when a group of willing and strong caregivers cannot safely transfer someone who uses a wheelchair. (I cringe when I witness well-intentioned people lift a person in a wheelchair up or down stairs. When a person is a wheelchair user, appropriate transportation and alternate ways in and out of buildings or up and down stairs must be considered when there is no ramp.)

Supplies

The cost of incontinence supplies—including disposables, catheters, wipes, gloves, skin protection, and other personal care needs—whether the person is at home or in a care community are considerable. It is often economically feasible to order incontinence supplies in bulk from home delivery companies like HDIS (www.hdis.com) or Disposables Delivered (www.disposablesdelivered.com). It is better to pay attention to the amount of absorbency, not the price. A cheaper, less absorbent product means more changes per day. In a care community, an added cost may depend on how many changes the care receiver requires per twenty-four hours. Many care communities charge for both the product and the number of times a person has to be changed or toileted.

My father was discharged from an acute rehab facility to a well-regarded Connecticut nursing home before I became an aware family caregiver, able to manage his care in our home with assistance. At that time, the cost was a mere $8,000 per month—in 1993! I had not yet found my way to a geriatric care manager for guidance. My father was incontinent due to paralysis. Little did I know then that the "free" incontinence product used in most facilities is poor quality, and therefore less absorbent. A poor-quality, less absorbent product requires frequent changes, which are rarely done in care settings. A urine-soaked product leads to skin breakdown and bedsores. Repeated changes throughout the day and night add to the cost of care, whether in a private setting or a care facility.

A considerable cost of supplies now because of coronavirus is for masks, disposable clothing, gloves, and face shields. Both family and paid caregivers in the home and beyond need to follow protocols for preventing the spread of the virus.

Downsizing, Moving, Relocation

Hiring a moving or downsizing specialist costs money, but it can be the path of least resistance when the need for care arises. When a loved one is moved to a new care setting, many family caregivers assume that the move will be permanent. The reality is that our loved one's first "move" may not be permanent. As they travel through different levels of care, whether at home or in a custodial setting, more moves may be necessary. Often, repeated moves are done to reduce the cost of care. Still, whether it's the initial downsizing from a home, or moving from a single room to a shared suite to reduce cost, or to a new floor, anticipate that there will be a cost.

My friend Sharon's mother died as I was penning these pages. Sharon lives in New England, and her mother lived in a continuing care community many states away. Sharon was her oldest living adult child. Her mother, who died at one hundred, had been the keeper of family heirlooms and treasures. Sharon didn't need or want many of the items, except for a large framed painting. She had no interest in cut glass, Wedgwood dinnerware, silver and silver-plated bowls and serving dishes, linens, and all the other furnishings that marked a woman of good taste and hence, good upbringing. Sharon was overwhelmed just thinking about clearing out her mother's home and having to attend to all of the matters that accompany a loved one's death. I suggested that Sharon use the services of a geriatric care manager, who referred her to a senior move manager,[5] who in turn coordinated the sale of her mother's home and goods and arranged to send special items that Sharon wanted to keep.

As an only child, I inherited linen from my mother and two aunts who didn't have any children. So I had linen, china, silverware, and furniture. While these items are lovely and were cherished by my mother and aunts, it took me a while to realize that I could not be the keeper of the "stuff." I learned this lesson after moving that stuff from Washington, DC—from my parent's home and my two aunts' homes—to my own family's home in New York. Then, my husband was called to a ministry or position in Washington, DC, which meant moving the stuff back again. First, I moved it all to the house that we rented for a year. Then I moved it to the house where we now live. Moving furniture multiple times is inefficient and costly: a lesson learned that I freely share with the families in my care. Now much of the stuff has been donated or trashed (yes, trashed).

Clothing

Family caregivers should keep in mind that a loved one's dignity is often related to how they present themselves to others. The reality of aging is that clothes get ruined, lost, or become ill-fitting. Loved ones need adaptive clothing if they use a wheelchair or if they have limited range of motion in their arms; such clothing is a worthwhile investment and can enhance quality of life. Companies worth mentioning that specialize in adaptive clothing are Buck & Buck (www .buckandbuck.com) and Silvert's (www.silverts.com). Even

---

5. The National Association of Senior Move Managers (NASMM) is the leading membership organization for senior move managers; see www.nasmm.org.

regular clothes need to be replaced; Haband (www.haband .com) is an inexpensive source for both men and women.

My father was well-groomed and paid attention to his appearance. He wore heavily starched shirts with white undershirts; his shoes were always polished. He continued to want to be well-groomed, as a wheelchair user and amputee. I remember coming up with a creative way to adapt his pants to avoid having his pant legs knotted, as is often seen with amputees. The cost of a tailor was a necessity in our case. Most older people will have some degree of limited mobility and range of motion, often in the shoulders and arms. Putting on a coat or jacket or blouse can become challenging if the armhole isn't generous enough or the garment doesn't have enough give. The cost of adaptive clothing can be another unanticipated expense.

One time during my father's short-term stay in rehab, I was called by the assisted living facility because my father was refusing to go to the dining room. We had care meetings upon care meetings to explore my father's "resistance" in the common dining room. Finally, I discovered he was not going into a dining room wearing just an undershirt. His request to be dressed in one of his starched shirts went unheeded. He told me that the caregivers said there was no need for him to use up his nicely pressed shirts because he was only going to the dining room! What a disregard for a person's preference.

Scott's mother had been a resident at an assisted living community in Washington, DC, and Scott lived in Massachusetts. As her memory declined and her money dwindled, Scott made plans to move her to Massachusetts. Scott's mother, despite dementia, was always well-coifed; she had a variety of wigs, always wore makeup, pearls, and earrings. I arranged for her move to Massachusetts by train with a professional caregiver. It was a long ride with an early morning departure, but still more appropriate than traveling by air or car.

Some time later, I got an e-mail from Scott:

> I want to let you know that my mother passed away this week. She went peacefully and comfortably. I can't thank you enough for all you did for us. Your plan was pure genius and the execution precise. I give you five stars!

I am certain that the eight-hour train ride from Washington to Boston was the "pure genius" that Scott complimented. I gave much attention to dressing his mother in the way that she preferred, even for the long train ride. As the orchestrator of the move, I made sure that she wore her false eyelashes and was dressed in a matching ensemble, adorned with pearls and the "right" wig. It was important that Scott's mom presented in the way that she would have if she could have done it herself. Plus, she was accompanied on the trip by her favorite caregiver.

Meals and Dietary Supplements

Medicare sometimes covers special dietary supplements, but only when "medically necessary." For example, cranberry juice (often recommended to help manage urinary tract infections) in bulk can add up to a significant expense. Even over-the-counter medications can add to the cost of care, but are often overlooked as an expense; instead, we tend to focus on the cost of prescribed medications.

My client, eighty-six-year-old Gertrude, was one of many clients who insisted on remaining in her own home, despite living in a two-story house. Not one of her four children lived nearby. Each had tried unsuccessfully to get her to move closer to one of them. Fiercely independent,

Gertrude did well caring for herself. She was compliant with medications, but couldn't easily prepare her own meals. I suggested to Gertrude and her family that they consider using a delivery service for fully prepared meals. Mom's Meals (www.momsmeals.com), for example, delivers fully prepared refrigerated meals, including special offerings such as pureed foods. They offer nationwide delivery. There are other companies, also. Family caregivers often find that daily meal preparation is one of the primary stressors in caring for a loved one. But meal delivery can be another cost. Many communities offer free meals and delivery; for example, see www.mealsonwheelsamerica.org. However, this arrangement isn't always appropriate.

I learned a lesson working with Bertha, then 101 years old. She lived at home with private, live-in care. Bertha had several allergies, as is often the case, especially with older people. Eldercare-givers must be vigilant to any changes. Bertha was delivered meals that included fruit and Ensure. After one delivery, Bertha began to have loose stools. I noticed that there was a different brand to replace Ensure and I called the organization that delivered the food. I quizzed the organization's nutritionist about the replacement. I remember her insisting, "The substitute for Ensure has exactly the same ingredients as Ensure." I recall clearly checking the label myself with a magnifying glass, and listed as the last ingredient in the substitute was soy— exactly the ingredient that Bertha was allergic to!

Be careful that any food donation or delivery service is appropriate for your loved one.

Furniture and Equipment

The cost of replacement and new furniture must be considered as part of eldercare-giving. A reclining chair, a larger TV, better lighting, or a bedside commode might be needed to enhance quality of life and to help the person who is providing hands-on care. Too often, caregivers struggle to provide bedside care without a conveniently located bedside table. I've also seen caregivers strain their backs to give bed care because the bed is too low. An electric hospital bed that raises and lowers is essential for care and safety. However, only under certain circumstances is an electric bed covered by insurance. Hospital beds and appropriate mattresses can be bought online, but be careful. Should the bed need to be repaired, the process can be cumbersome and also private pay. In the long run it may be best to rent a hospital bed. Shop around.

Armless chairs have to be replaced with chairs that have arms. For a frail person with mobility issues, a chair without arms is a safety hazard—there's no leverage to help and getting up from one is risky.

For comfort and safety, a wheelchair and its cushion and support should be fitted to the individual. On average, a manual wheelchair for daily use costs between $1,000 and $2,000, excluding any special add-ons. The cost of a motorized wheelchair varies widely from $7,000 upwards, sometimes exceeding $25,000 with bells and whistles. I recently was able to get a client who has Parkinson's disease a motorized wheelchair as a rental. However, if she had had to pay for the chair, it would have cost $17,000. The motorized wheelchair gives her the independence that she would not have in a manual wheelchair that she cannot propel herself. A properly fitting wheelchair is not only a quality-of-life matter, but also a health concern because the body should be properly aligned. Another hidden cost in buying a wheelchair is the carrier for the car, especially if the wheelchair is electric or if it is a scooter.

My father's nearly six-month stay in the acute rehab center is the source of my knowledge about wheelchairs. I had to learn about wheelchair seating clinics and seating systems. When caring for a wheelchair user, we must make sure our loved one is comfortable. One of my pet peeves is seeing someone slumped over or clearly ill-positioned in a wheelchair. That doesn't have to be the case. Ask at any rehabilitation center or rehabilitation hospital for referral to a seating clinic. At a seating clinic, the person's pressure points can be measured and a proper wheelchair size, frame, and cushion can be determined. Sometimes Medicare will cover the cost of a wheelchair fitting; often they do not.

Good, comfortable, appropriate seating and the right mattress for the hospital bed are both important and essential expenditures for a loved one's well-being, as are canes and walkers, which come in various styles and heights. As caregivers, we must make sure the equipment is appropriate for the person using it. A cane needs to be the right height and the handle and base need to be secure. One cane does not fit all.

Ronald (not his real name) is seventy-four and morbidly obese. I have followed his care for years. He needs a hip replacement. He can no longer walk. His caregivers must use a Hoyer lift to move him into his oversize wheelchair from his bed. His family asked me to assess his situation. When I visited him, I noticed that he was sitting in a wheelchair with a cushion less than one inch thick. He told me that before he got the cushion, he had been sitting directly on the sling seat of the wheelchair. Immediately, with consultation with the occupational therapist,

I suggested ordering a special cushion—a ROHO cushion—for him. The therapist had not suggested it because she assumed that since it would be a private-pay item, the family wouldn't want to pay for it. Yet, she knew that Ronald wasn't comfortable and sacrificed his comfort for cost, which wasn't significant. Ronald told me that he didn't realize how uncomfortable he was on the thin cushion until he sat on his new, carefully fitted ROHO cushion.

If the plan is for the individual to *age in place*, their house will have to be retrofitted, which extends beyond installing grab bars. Universal or accessible design is an approach in which buildings, products, and environments are accessible to everyone, including people with special needs. If the renovation is done correctly using universal design, it may be unnecessary to move an aging loved one from the house. A ramp may need to be installed or a doorway widened to accommodate a wheelchair. Sinks can be lowered for easier and safer use. A roll-in shower or a walk-in tub is useful.

Vision aids, hearing aids, and hearing aid batteries are another overlooked cost. The website www.independent living.com is a popular source for low vision aids, hearing aids, healthcare and mobility products, and assistive technology for independent living. Eyeglasses, which are often misplaced by people with memory issues, can add up when they need to be replaced. Keep in mind that there is an array of assistive devices, such as caption telephones, tracking devices, and monitors, that are not covered by insurance.

As caregivers, we must keep an eye on our loved one's comfort and our own comfort, as well as the ease of care. We often improvise, but then should check to be sure that our improvisation is appropriate. I have seen so many caregivers use an "egg crate" pad on a chair pad or a makeshift ramp, not to code. It has been determined that this may contribute to pressure sores, particularly if the person lacks chair mobility. Safer and more appropriate devices and aids are widely available for seating and many other needs. We have to resist makeshift approaches that may prove to be harmful, even if less costly.

One-on-One Care

As I guide clients through the long-term care maze, I prepare them for the possibility that their loved one who requires long-term care may likely require one-to-one care at some point. One-on-one care is always private pay. The widely held assumption is that when needed, a hospital, assisted living community, or nursing home will provide one-on-one care. Be advised: 24/7 care does not mean one-on-one care. When a loved one is hospitalized, they may need a bedside advocate or a one-to-one caregiver, especially if they have a cognitive deficit, are hearing or visually impaired, or are immobile. There's a cost.

Many families assume from the high cost of care in assisted living that one-on-one care is covered. Nothing could be further from reality. Assisted living only includes limited hands-on care. So, increased agitation, night roaming, frequent bed turning, and other factors may require one-on-one care within that care setting.

As the trend for aging in place continues, the demand for caregivers will continue to increase. According to the most recent *Occupational Outlook Handbook*:

> Employment of home health aides and personal care aides is projected to grow 36 percent from 2018 to 2028, much faster than the average for all occupations. As the baby-boom population ages and the elderly population

grows, the demand for the services of home health aides and personal care aides will continue to increase.[6]

This, of course, signals that the hourly wage of a professional caregiver will increase as well. With a rise in both the scarcity and the cost of paid caregivers, family and informal caregivers may have to fill in the gaps. Be careful, however, and adhere to employment laws. Do not pay "under the table"; it is against the law.

Legal arrangements are available. They go by a variety of names: support services agreement, eldercare contract, family care or caregiver contract, or personal care agreement. They should be done for anyone who provides care to the loved one. The website www.caregiver.org is a good resource for a list of the components necessary for such an agreement. Publication 926, "Household Employer's Tax Guide" (www.irs.gov), offers guidelines for employing a household worker.

At the start of my caregiving journey with my father, two friends—one an estate attorney, Frank; the other an attorney, Marsha, who is also a priest—came to the house. (I was recovering from major surgery and couldn't manage going out, nor was there any immediate way to get my father out of the house to Frank's law office.) Frank, the estate attorney, had created a personal care agreement, among other documents. The care agreement outlined duties and compensation. While I trusted Frank, I was uncomfortable with having a contract with my father to pay me as his family caregiver. However, I came to understand the importance

---

6. U.S. Bureau of Labor Statistics, U.S. Department of Labor, *Occupational Outlook Handbook*, Home Health Aides and Personal Care Aides, accessed May 7, 2020, https://www.bls.gov/ooh/healthcare/home-health-aides-and-personal-care-aides.htm.

and benefit of having a personal care agreement. In my situation, I realized that the monthly compensation and duties in the agreement were a formal outline. In the years that ensued, my father never paid me as such. However, if a Medicaid spend-down had been the plan, the payments to me would have been a deduction. Of course, I would have had to report those earnings on my tax return. I recommend that each caregiver, whether family or informal, insist on having a personal care agreement from their loved one separate and apart from any kind of estate document. Many templates and instructions that advise what features, services, and provisions the agreement should contain are available online.

Care Levels

As a family caregiver, know your loved one's level of care. An effective family eldercare giver must understand and accept the level of care their loved one requires. How much help does your loved one need with activities of daily life (ADLs)? This is especially important to understand if your loved one is in a large long-term care facility or even a smaller group home. Determining a level of care is state specific. One assisted living facility might have five care levels, each at a different daily rate. The range can be wide—for example, at one urban assisted living community the rate for 2019 ranged from $30 per day (lowest care level) to $115 per day (highest level of assistance). These amounts are on top of the basic room and board cost.

Pills, Pills Everywhere, and Never a One Was Taken Correctly

In assisted living, the cost of medication management depends on how many times medications are given in a twenty-four-hour period. Basically, the more pills, the more the daily add-on to the basic cost of room and board. For care at home, it is wise to budget for a medication management system. There are a range of options. A pill box should be carefully selected to match the care receiver's cognition, sight, and dexterity. The one-style-fits-all container commonly found in drugstores is not adequate or appropriate for most people living with cognitive dissonance or any other disability. The appropriate box is also one that fits the user's meds. Whether pills are sorted into a pillbox with compartments, blister-packed, or given through a technology-assisted pill dispensary system, a medication management system is necessary.

Ten years ago, Edwina was a long-distance caregiver for her mother. She searched for help and found me. Edwina lived in Maryland and her mother lived in New York. At the time, I commuted weekly between the two cities, so I was able to be physically present for both Edwina in Maryland and for her mother in New York. On my first visit with her mother, I saw the usual mash-up of pill bottles. I asked Edwina how her mother managed her meds because I was confident that her mother had some cognitive challenges. Edwina told me that she called her mother weekly and told her how to fill the pillbox. Plus, Edwina assumed that the twice-weekly visits from her mother's home health aide were an effective way to monitor her mother's meds, but that responsibility was not one that an aide who was not certified as a med tech or licensed to handle medications should have been doing.

I've visited many homes and I've seen pill bottles lined up like trophies, a mingling of current and out-of-date medications. I have also seen medication hoarding. Medication mistakes are common and can cause harm or even death. We must make sure an appropriate medication management system is in place. The cost of hiring a professional, usually a nurse, for regular visits to set up medications may be necessary to monitor medications and to oversee prescription refills. Medication management is one of the least attended to aspects of eldercare in the home and among the most dangerous, if not managed properly.

I've asked countless clients, "Does your mother take her meds?" Often the answer is, "Yes." My follow-up is, "Are you assuming that she does, or do you actually see her take her meds?" Upon probing, the family caregiver most often assumes the meds have been taken and depends on their loved one to self-report. Assume nothing.

Behind the Wheel: A Helpful Resource

Driving is linked to independence. As a loved one ages, a caregiver must be on the lookout for driving problems. When a driving concern arises, a family caregiver should check for a company or facility that can conduct a comprehensive driving assessment; an acute rehab hospital is often a good resource. For example, the driving assessment program offered at the National Rehabilitation Hospital in Washington, DC, is excellent. The cost varies, but a comprehensive assessment ranges between $350 and $750 in the DC area. Since driving is one of the areas that causes much discord between a family caregiver and a loved one, the cost of a neutral party's assessment is worth the investment. The assessment has five components.

1. **Clinical Driving Evaluation (Pre-driving):** A review of medical and driving history, including an assessment of physical abilities, cognitive functioning, road knowledge, vision, and reaction time.

2. **Behind-the-Wheel Evaluation:** An assessment of driving ability and an introduction to equipment and techniques that can assist in maximizing driving performance. Specific driving routes have been designed to give a clear snapshot of abilities.

3. **Report and Recommendations:** Once evaluation is completed, the entire assessment is discussed and recommendations provided. The report and recommendations will indicate whether a person can return to driving.

4. **Vehicle Fittings:** If the report shows it is safe to continue driving but vehicle fittings are recommended, the vehicle is modified to place all controls relative to the person's driving position and abilities.

5. **Final Road Test Preparation:** This ensures that the driver is proficient and comfortable navigating regular driving routes with the adaptive controls.

Directing a care receiver to a driving assessment program instead of simply taking away the keys, which can cause consternation between a family caregiver and their loved one, gives the loved one some sense of agency in the process.

I worked with a couple who were both cognitively impaired but high-functioning to some degree. However, they both had poor judgment about many life issues. Both had impaired executive functioning. Their adult children lived far away. Delores, the wife, told me that she was afraid when her husband was driving, but she insisted that if he went no more than two or three miles to the store, for example, he was fine. Despite her misgivings, she insisted that he drive her to her club meetings and church because she believed she had no other way to get there. Her husband had been returned home several times by the police after becoming lost. Once, she didn't know where he was for hours. And he had numerous fender-benders.

I recommended a full driving assessment. For the Nichols, the cost was $600 for each one. The report was submitted to the Department of Motor Vehicles. Neither of their driver's licenses was renewed and one was revoked. As a result, the couple agreed to have a paid caregiver to drive them in their car.

Senior-Serving Professionals

Senior-serving professionals offer a smorgasbord of services and are knowledgeable about the array of aging issues—social, medical, health, financial, and legal. These professionals are certified and their expertise can save time and money in the long run. The general public has been slow in becoming aware of these professionals, largely because their existence is often discovered by word-of-mouth when the family is in the middle of the crisis. Senior-serving professionals include geriatric care managers, elder law attorneys, financial planners, senior move specialists, daily money managers, and geriatricians. There's a cost, but advice and expertise comes with a cost. Consult a tax attorney, as some services may be tax deductible.

The Bottom Line

Long-term care—wherever it is delivered—takes a chunk of money. Cutting corners may end up costing more emotional and financial currency than might otherwise be necessary. It may also compromise quality of life. When the rainy day comes and we need long-term care, preparation and planning are the keys to quality living. Steve Weisman, in his book *A Guide to Elder Planning: Everything You Need* to *Know to Protect Yourself Legally and Financially*, writes, "Studies predict the cost of nursing homes will approach $200,000 per year by year 2030 when the last of the baby boomers will be reaching age sixty-five."[7]

Let me offer a very recent example. A young senior I've followed for nearly five years died from the COVID-19 virus. He lived in an AL community. He had advanced dementia and for the last several years received one-to-one care, which his son felt was essential for his well-being. I asked the son, who was fortunately financially secure and able to private pay, exactly how much he spent on average each year for his father's care. Without hesitation, he said, "Two hundred thousand a year!" Shocking, but from real life.

Professional caregivers are in a position to broaden the thinking of family caregivers and guide them toward long-term care arrangements beyond the nursing home or assisted living facility that may be more financially sustainable. Therein lie opportunities to unpack the cost of long-term care and devise creative ways that long-term care can be funded.

The rainy day comes with a cost.

7. Steve Weisman, *A Guide to Elder Planning: Everything You Need to Know to Protect Yourself Legally and Financially* (Upper Saddle River, NJ: Pearson Education, 2004), 150.

CHAPTER TEN

I Don't Want to Live to Be a Hundred!

Sharon, my friend of over forty years, always remembers my birthday. She has called me every August for our entire friendship. On my last birthday, for some reason, I decided to call Sharon before she called me. She was surprised. I told her she had been on my mind. The first thing that I asked was how she was doing. And before I could utter anything else, she said, "I don't want to live to be a hundred!"

Sharon and I first met when we were in our thirties. We were both married and full of professional vigor. She was a parish priest and I was a very serious academic. Besides being a great friend and confidant, she was our son Guillermo's "fairy godmother." Sharon adored Guillermo. He had no idea that they weren't related, despite their racial difference. Sharon indulged him like a fairy godmother should and she gave him free rein under her watchful eye. I have a treasured photo of two-and-a-half-year-old Guillermo carefully snuffing out candles at Sharon's dinner table. The joke is that Sharon's nurturing Guillermo by allowing him to snuff out candles likely paved the way for his becoming an acolyte. Since I have no siblings, Sharon is both sister and friend. She is also my caregiver of the "pastoral sort."

"I'm glad you called," Sharon said. "I need your care!"

I asked a few questions and finally Sharon told me about her mother's upcoming one hundredth birthday celebration, which was causing Sharon anxiety and triggering conflicted feelings. She and her mother didn't have a compatible relationship. Sharon said she needed some caregiving from me to help her through the mixed feelings about her mother's birthday and the party that was planned by her mother's friends, residents at the life care community where her mother had lived for years. Sharon said that she needed pastoral care of the "eldercare sort." We laughed. It was my turn to be Sharon's caregiver. The tables turned, and now I provided care to the person who had been my caregiver during the years when I was entangled between my parents, my professional life, and my husband and son.

Sharon's mother passed away about three weeks after her birthday. Sharon lives in Vermont and her mother lived in Maryland. Over a few weeks, Sharon made several trips back and forth from Vermont. In my role now as Sharon's caregiver, I suggested that she enlarge her team of caregivers and contact a colleague in Maryland, who is an aging life care professional like me, for hands-on care and support as she navigated her mother's end-of-life care. I continued as an informal caregiver through daily calls with suggestions to help her through this phase of the journey. Like many eldercare-givers, it takes a bit of nudging to reach out for help. I had to nudge Sharon and insist that she not wait to call my colleague. Later, Sharon told me that my nudge was what she needed because contacting a care manager, to her mind, underscored the finality of her relationship with her mother.

My colleague was superb and helped and guided Sharon before and after her mother's death. When Sharon told me that she dreaded having to spend a night in her mother's condo after her mother's death, I suggested that she contact a senior move manager through my colleague and turn over what she was dreading having to do. Sharon is now a believer in the efficacy of using senior-serving professionals. Prior to her experience, she knew that I did eldercare, but she had no idea how indispensable an eldercare advisor can be.

Over the years, Sharon has talked to me about the troubled relationship that she had with her mother and gave me permission to tell her story. I was better prepared to provide caregiving for this matter because of recent training in psychotherapy and aging through the Washington School of Psychiatry and in psychoanalysis through the Washington Baltimore Center for Psychoanalysis. I suspect that much of the disconnect between Sharon and her mother was a result of her mother not being attuned to Sharon when Sharon was a child. It is likely that her mother did not give Sharon the kind of care and nurturing that she needed. This is not intended as criticism; as one person put it to me, "We can only give what we have."

When Sharon's only sibling, a brother, passed away, she became her mother's sole family member, except for Sharon's daughter and son-in-law. Sharon had not lived near her mother since leaving home for college. After living through her mother's decline, Sharon told me that she did not want to live to be a centenarian. It was apparent to me that Sharon's "aging model" was based on her mother's aging. I used the best of my knowledge about aging and told Sharon it is usually not really the chronological age that we reject, but the negative way that aging is viewed or experienced in this society. I stressed to her that she could choose to age differently; it was a choice, even if she were to face a debilitating illness. Sharon said that she had never considered aging well or aging positively. She realized that the only way she thought about growing old was as an infirmed person, like her mother. Sharon appreciated the revised way of thinking about growing old. I reminded her that her own relationship with her daughter was a loving one and she was an attuned mother.

I wrote this chapter a week after Sharon's mother's memorial service. I continued to call Sharon daily to check in. Mainly, we talked about fun stuff: the Eileen Fisher clothes we both enjoy wearing, and being proud mothers of successful adult children. Blake, Sharon's daughter, is completing her PhD at Princeton, and Guillermo is an accomplished musician and house band member on CBS's *The Late Late Show with James Corden*. Sharon grieves, but she told me she would not have been able to come so soon to our "fun place" had she not had the care and support of a team of senior-serving professionals.

CHAPTER ELEVEN

Mr. Jackson's Potato Salad and Aunt Ruth's Kale Salad

Treat others the way that they want to be treated. That is the platinum rule of caregiving. Embrace the "otherness" to the fullest extent possible. Caregiving calls us very often to put aside what we believe to be "right" or to put aside our own preferences.

In one cultural tradition, licking one's fingers during a meal is a sign that the meal was enjoyed and appreciated. In another culture, licking one's fingers is bad manners. Caregiving means being attuned to the person we are caring for. That awareness must be the foundation of effective and loving caregiving—and that just may be the hardest part of caregiving. Being attuned to the other isn't a concrete caregiving task, like giving medicine, helping with personal care, or accompanying a loved one to a doctor's appointment. Being attuned is hard work, just not physical work.

Caregiving requires a particular kind of competency: being able to put aside our own notions of the way things must or should be. Effective and loving caregiving is the willingness to put our own notions in the background, easy to say, hard to do. Take, for example, meal preparation. The easy task is cooking the meal. The more difficult work is honoring the specific preferences of the care receiver.

One of the things that I did for my father as one of his caregivers was to fix some of his meals. Often, in doing so, I was pushed to my wit's end. That's when I called my father "Mr. Jackson," not "Daddy." My father loved potato salad. One day, he asked me to fix some. I knew to ask him exactly what ingredients I should use because he liked a certain taste. He told me the ingredients: mayonnaise, yellow mustard, sweet relish, onions, eggs, apple cider vinegar, and some sugar. He instructed that the potato salad should be refrigerated overnight to meld the flavors. And he said, "Remember to rinse the potatoes in cold water after they are boiled. And then cut up the potatoes."

I did everything Mr. Jackson requested, overnight chilling and all. I followed his instructions exactly. The next day when I served my father my carefully crafted potato salad, before even tasting it he said, "The potatoes are too big." Imagine my frustration and anger, after jumping through all the hoops trying to satisfy him. I was furious. But the incident taught me an important caregiving lesson. Accept that it's likely impossible to get it completely right, or even nearly right. And accept that sometimes it will be completely wrong.

For my father to enjoy potato salad, I realized that he had to participate directly in its preparation in some way. I was so busy being on task that I failed to recognize that my father could easily have participated in preparing the salad by cutting up the potatoes to the size that he preferred.

As caregivers, we must know that we have power to draw the line. As caregivers, we must also be mindful to know our limit. Otherwise, anger, frustration, and compassion fatigue will result.

Often we do more than we need to do. Sometimes it's easier and faster to do something for the care receiver rather than to stand by and watch them struggle. Letting them complete a task takes patience, but it helps to send a message to the care receiver: "You may be sick, but there are things that you can do for yourself." I learned from my mother how it is possible to find a small but important thing for someone to be engaged in and to do. Be creative.

As a child, I loved watching my mother sew on the machine. As she sewed, it was my job to pick the pins up off the floor and stick them into the cushion. That task kept me busy and I felt good because I was helping and doing something. As caregivers, we must be creative and find ways to involve the care receiver, even in the smallest way. This fosters self-respect and reinforces the value of giving back. No one gets a free ride—even the frailest, sickest person.

Another lesson: we must resist being lured into arguments. For caregivers, it's easy to fall into this trap. A big argument could have ensued if I had tried to convince my father that the size of the potatoes didn't matter or that he should be thankful that he even had potatoes for a salad. Was my father being unreasonable? Maybe yes, maybe no. The advice to caregivers, whether family or professional, is if the person you are caring for wants water, don't give them wine.

Be aware that sometimes we will not get it right; we will get it not quite right or not right at all. Regardless, we must respect a person's cultural traditions, personal preferences, and values. Remember it is not always possible to make the person happy or content. I often hear from family caregivers who say things like, "I just want to make my mother/ father/husband/wife happy." Do what you can, but don't whip yourself into a frenzy or go on a guilt trip.

My mother's youngest sibling of ten children, my aunt Ruth, is almost ninety years old. She is in reasonably good health, walks, travels, uses a computer, and, so far, has had no car accidents. Her nails are always well manicured. She lives with her son and daughter-in-law in her own well-equipped and comfortable in-law suite. But, she has arthritis in her hands. She doesn't complain about any pain. Yet, on one visit, she asked me, in the most pleading voice possible, to make her the kale salad I once served for a party that she attended.

"Why can't you make the salad?" I asked. The recipe was not complex.

"I can't cut up the kale," she said. Instead of giving in to my aunt's pleas, I took my iPad and showed her a variety of kitchen aids and cutting knives especially designed for people with arthritis.

Perhaps what was really behind her plea was that she was admitting she was tired of having to cook. That is when I suggested she look into Mom's Meals (www.moms meals.com), one of the national meal delivery companies that prepares, packages, and delivers meals. The company has a range of menus that are suitable for various diets and preferences.

"Oh," my aunt Ruth said, "I didn't know that there was such a thing." A few weeks later when I checked in, she said, "Oh, I love Mom's Meals. They make mealtime so much easier."

That's an example of effective eldercare. I didn't get manipulated. Nor did I take a guilt trip. I found a way to help her solve her problem, not just for the time I was there to physically help her, but for the future.

CHAPTER TWELVE

You Don't Owe Your Loved One Your Well-Being

In her book *The Courage to Grow Old*, Barbara Cawthorne Crafton, an Episcopal priest, says that when she is in a caregiving-pastoral role with someone who is trying to take care of an aging parent, one of the first questions that she asks is, "What is troubling you the most?"

Crafton says that she usually gets one of two answers: the consequences of a certain promise that was made to a parent or a loved one, or wanting to make their loved one "happy." "I have seen many adult children rise to the occasion of their parents' final illness, even when the relationship was not at all an easy one."[1] I especially appreciate the cautionary note that she gives to adult children—that they don't owe their parent (and, I add, their loved one) the sacrifice of their own well-being. "Honor thy father and thy mother doesn't mean enabling our parents' denial of the facts of their lives."[2]

---

1. Barbara Cawthorne Crafton, *The Courage to Grow Old* (Harrisburg, PA: Morehouse, 2014), 6.

2. Crafton, *Courage to Grow Old*, 7.

In my eldercare practice, I have had countless adult children tell me, "I just want them to be happy," when speaking of their parent or loved one. Equally troubling for an adult child is when their loved one needs a higher level of care because of dementia or a chronic illness. I also hear, "My mother told me never to put her in a nursing home." As the caregiver's caregiver, I try to ease them toward freedom from guilt.

I learned a lesson that I pass on to caregivers: you cannot make everyone happy. You can wish happiness for a loved one, but it is impossible to create happiness for someone else.

My mother told me over and over about a promise that she made as a teenager, which she was ultimately held captive by. As the eldest of ten of her siblings, she was the responsible big sister. Her mother died in childbirth with my mother's youngest sibling. My mother was fifteen. Her father was killed when my mother was sixteen. Her grandparents reared her and her siblings. "On his deathbed," my mother said, "Grandpa asked me to be a mother for my siblings." My mother carried that heavy mantle of responsibility all her life.

Given my mother's early life experience with death, dying, and illness, and then the death of my baby sister and my mother's recounting of the promise she made to her grandfather, I was quite young when I became "death aware." And I experienced the consequences of my mother's continued questioning about whether she did a good job as she had promised her grandfather. What a burden my mother carried all of her life. Her promise impacted me as well since my mother recounted that promise time and time again.

Guilt is among the hardest issues for a family caregiver to overcome. Help and support are required to free a caregiver.

Even though I knew that I had done all that was possible for my parents, there was still a haunting nag whether there was any more that I could have done.

Once when my mother was in the hospital she asked me to help position her on the bed pan. I was about sixteen years old. I helped, but as soon as she finished, I ran from her room overcome by the smell of urine that was tainted with an antibiotic that caused her urine to smell a particular way. My mother's hospital roommate followed me as I ran from the room. She told me it was unfair and inappropriate for my mother to ask me to help with her bed pan when she was in the hospital with nurses and professional caregivers. Had it not been for my mother's roommate, I likely would have carried guilt for abandoning my mother when she was in need.

As caregivers, we must learn to accept that there are things that we will be able to do and other things that we will not. Keep the Serenity Prayer in mind: "God, grant me the serenity to accept the things I cannot change, courage to change the things I can, and wisdom to know the difference." As caregivers, we should not promise to do something that circumstances may well not allow us to fulfill.

Despite being a huge and challenging burden, caregiving can be a life-fulfilling experience like no other. Like parenting, caregiving can get easier and less stressful with practice, instruction, and preparation. For example, make sure that powers of attorney are in place for you and your loved one; compile your loved one's medical history; create a list of your loved one's medical and non-medical providers, as well as a current list of medications; and make copies of insurance cards. Gathering all of this will make caregiving lighter, once the effort has been expended. "Stay ready so you don't have to get ready" is the rule I recommend. Stay as much ahead of the crisis as is possible.

Anticipate. Accept that aging, most often, is accompanied by declining health. Care over cure is to be remembered. Besides my oft-used adage, "Stay ready so you don't have to get ready," there are some basic skills to become effective caregivers for our aging loved ones. I offer two here in particular.

One, practice patience. Resist engaging in battles. Use humor. And practice what dementia experts call "therapeutic fibbing." I like the way Crafton describes this skill:

> [There has to be a] willingness to ride with them [the care recipient who is memory impaired] upon the rolling sea of their shifting perceptions, rather than demanding that they endorse the categories of a world they no longer experience. . . . [It] is more loving than the truth-telling we admire in more ordinary times.[3]

It is controversial; however, I believe when it's used for good intent it is appropriate.

Second, let go of having to be right. If your loved one says that she sees her mother and the reality is her mother is dead, it is far more loving to say, "Tell me about her. What did she say to you?" instead of, "Your mother died years ago!" Let me share an example from real life.

As I was writing these words, I got a call from Margaret, a seasoned and mature caregiver, or so I thought. Margaret called to complain about June, whose daughters had hired Margaret to help their mother shower and dress and to accompany her to breakfast. The daughters wanted Margaret to spend about four hours each morning with their mother, who is in her nineties and lives in a supportive care community. Her dementia has advanced. Every day when Margaret

---

3. Crafton, *Courage to Grow Old*, 42.

arrives, June tells her to leave because her daughter will help her. Margaret feels rejected. She called me to complain. She not only said that she feels rejected, but she complained that June was uncooperative and resistant to care. Margaret said she was frustrated and hurt by June's constant dismissal of her. At her wit's end with June, Margaret called one of the daughters—right in front of her.

Margaret's call to the daughter was an expression of her need to prove that June was wrong and that Margaret, not the daughter, was the one who helped her in the morning.

Margaret told me June's belligerent behavior meant she could not do her job. And June's insistence that one of her daughters would do her morning care rattled Margaret to annoyance. Margaret reinforced her position by saying that the staff agreed that June was disagreeable and refused to face facts.

I was disheartened to listen to Margaret's characterization of June and the battle between Margaret and June over who was right and who was wrong. Despite Margaret's extensive training as a professional caregiver, she forgot an essential rule: caregiving isn't the time to prove that you are right—especially for someone with a cognitive impairment or who is chronically ill and in pain. As caregivers, we are often provoked and go into a battle. Resist. Practice patience, humility, and humor.

The ministry of caregiving takes patience to the nth degree. My husband, who has accompanied me on my own family and professional journey as a caregiver and caregiver's caregiver, constantly reminds me that to be effective in this ministry, we must be mindful and practice a non-anxious presence. We will not always succeed every day, but we can continue to practice discipline, hard work, and mindfulness.

CHAPTER THIRTEEN

Stay Ready

The writings of two theologians, Verna Dozier and Anne Rowthorn, undergird my embracing of eldercare as ministry.

The late Verna Dozier's book *The Authority of the Laity*[1] (co-authored with Celia Hahn) was published in 1982, the year that I joined the staff at 815. Dozier was a laywoman in the Episcopal Church. Her writing guided me toward an understanding of my own authority within the institutional church and in the world. The compact book of only forty-one pages explores a theology that the church is not a mere institution, but is about the authority of the People of God, given to them at baptism, to fully live their lives as followers of Jesus Christ.

Anne Rowthorn's *The Liberation of the Laity*[2] presents the theology by which all Christians discover their calling— their *ministry*. Rowthorn sets forth a "theology of the laity by the laity" rooted in the catechism from the Book of Common Prayer (BCP).

---

1. Verna Dozier and Celia Hahn, *The Authority of the Laity* (Durham, NC: The Alban Institute, 1982).

2. Anne Rowthorn, *The Liberation of the Laity* (Eugene, OR: Wipf and Stock, 2000).

Question: Who are the ministers of the Church?

Answer: The ministers of the Church are lay persons, bishops, priests, and deacons.[3]

The specific ministry of the laity is clear: "to represent Christ and his Church; to bear witness to him wherever they may be . . . according to gifts given them."[4]

I had an epiphany when I first read Rowthorn's description of the people who do everyday work as "saints." These are people she sees as Christ's representatives in the world. "[Saints] keep stable the fabric of the world,"[5] she says of laypeople who are employed in the occupations of the world. Rowthorn then cites "personal models"—artists, teachers, garage mechanics, babysitters, business execs, waitresses, trash collectors, maids, doctors, volunteers, auto mechanics, and a host of other people who toil and give daily.

Among the saints she mentions are the "church executives." And she includes my name as one of the saints who toils in that role. Me? A saint with a ministry? I was stunned to be cited. I was awakened to begin to see my work, in whatever form it takes, as a calling and as a ministry. And over the years, in a host of professional endeavors, I have come to understand that ministry takes many forms.

During this time when a pandemic is consuming the world, first-line care providers, nurses, doctors, professional caregivers, police officers, ambulance drivers, emergency responders, bus drivers, and countless oth-

---

3. Book of Common Prayer, 855.
4. BCP, 855.
5. Rowthorn, *Liberation of the Laity*, 80.

ers are saints who can't be compensated enough for the care they give. Each one of these caregivers is called to a ministry of caregiving, whether they consciously realize it as such.

A minister is someone who attends to the needs of another. A minister, then, is a servant. A minister is a giver. A minister is an agent. A minister is a caregiver.

Atul Gawande, a physician cited earlier in chapter 8, chronicles his own experience as a caregiver in his best seller, *Being Mortal*. In the book's final pages he writes what I've decided is the clarion call to the ministry of caregiving: "There comes a moment when responsibility shifts to someone else to decide what to do. . . . We're not prepared for that moment."[6]

I didn't think I was prepared to be the caregiver for my mother or my father or anyone else. As I look back to when our son was born, I can see my fear of being unprepared to be a caregiver as a mother.

We are often equipped in ways we're not aware of. Shelley is our adopted goddaughter, the daughter I never had. She's now in her mid-forties. I'll always be thankful to her for sharing some of the caregiving for my father. My father loved jazz. Shelley supplied him with tapes and CDs, and directed him to radio programs. When Shelley and I met, she was just out of college. I was her mentor in a program for recent college grads.

In the summer of 2003, Shelley asked me to go with her to find an apartment to rent. We went to apartment buildings, looked at shared arrangements, rooms in houses, and so forth. At one point, I suggested she look

---

6. Atul Gawande, *Being Mortal: Medicine and What Matters in the End* (New York: Henry Holt and Co., 2014), 252.

at a condo that was for sale in the neighborhood. I knew the listing agent. After lots of caregiving and coaching from me, she realized the financial advantage of buying a home rather than renting. But she was afraid to take on a mortgage, even though she had the income to support the purchase. She was fearful about taking on a loan because of past experiences in her family of origin. A loan was something to be avoided.

Both of us expected that I would be with her at the closing. However, on the day of the closing my father had to be taken to the emergency room. I was with him in the ambulance and in the emergency room. Shelley had to go to the closing without me, alone. She handled the closing, bought the condo, and now has substantial equity in her own place. Her need for a place to live overrode her fear, much like I had to override my fear in becoming my father's caregiver. Both of us found something within that gave us the courage to persevere and to take the plunge that we felt ill-equipped to do.

The thought of becoming and being a caregiver is more than daunting. It is a frightening moment when responsibility shifts to you to decide what to do. Caregiving can take many forms. When I was arranging my mother's memorial service, the then dean of Howard University's Divinity School, Lawrence Jones, suggested a book, *Final Gifts* by Maggie Callanan and Patricia Kelley. I will be forever grateful for his end-of-life caregiving. While the book focuses on death and dying, it has profound value for caregivers at any time along the caregiving journey.

It's hard to know how to help, what to do, what to say. Yet, if we know how to listen and what to look for, the person [who needs the care] can often supply the answers, letting us [the caregiver] know what they need to hear and express to allay their fears . . .[7]

On a recent visit with a family I have worked with for a decade but only see occasionally, I learned that Mrs. Ann, as she is called, had had several unobserved falls. She is ninety-two years old and lives by herself. As I greeted her, the first thing that she said was, "I am all broken down."

Her daughter and I, without thinking, both said, "Look at you. You're walking and you had no trouble getting out of the car!"

Reflecting on my visit the next day, I told Patrice, her daughter, that we needed to listen to what her mother was really saying. Reflecting, I am sure that Mrs. Ann was telling both of us in an indirect way that she herself realized that she was slowing down and didn't have the energy that she once had to move quickly. Fortunately, I had already suggested that she use a wheelchair and she did so as we moved about checking out a continuing care community. But, honestly, I suggested using the wheelchair for safety, not because I had actually listened to what Mrs. Ann was revealing. It's so easy to hear and react, but not to listen.

Caregiving Comes in Many Forms

Caregiving can be quiet. A caregiver can be a sitter, a visitor, a listener. A caregiver can simply be present and available.

Caregiving can be active. Assisting someone with activities of daily living, like dressing, meals, scheduling appointments, and so on. Shopping for a loved one, for example.

---

7. Maggie Callanan and Patricia Kelley, *Final Gifts: Understanding the Special Awareness, Needs, and Communications of the Dying* (New York: Simon and Schuster, 1992), 299.

Caregiving can be passive. A call to someone who needs care. Providing financial support for the on-site or paid caregiver. Sitting and listening.

Caregiving comes in many forms and ways. Whatever one's gift is, that gift can be used when a care need arises.

The Gospels of Mark, Matthew, and Luke all contain the account about Jesus's healing of Simon Peter's mother-in-law. I've listened to many sermons on the story, but I have yet to hear an exegesis that lifts the "other" caregiver in the biblical account into view. Jesus is the obvious caregiver, but there is another caregiver in the story.

Simon Peter's mother-in-law was in bed with a fever. Jesus was called to the woman's bedside by her family because they cared about her. They wanted Jesus to assist and comfort their loved one. It is not clear whether the family expected Jesus to heal her, but we can assume that they knew Jesus would provide some form of care. In the various accounts, Jesus leaned over and took her by the hand; Jesus touched her or came close to her as she lay in bed. Her family—the ones who called Jesus to their loved one's bedside—were her family caregivers. They were watchful, aware that it was time to call for assistance and care that they could not provide.

In the African American folk tradition, Jesus is often referred to as "Dr. Jesus." Jesus was the woman's professional caregiver. It's a watchful family caregiver who calls the doctor or an ambulance when in need of a professional caregiver, trained to give hands-on care.

The Gospel accounts tell us that the woman was cured—the fever left. Restored, she got up and began to serve. She, in turn, became a caregiver by preparing and serving a meal. She is the other caregiver.

The Care We Receive

I regard myself as a "caregiver's caregiver." Formally, one might call it the work of an applied gerontologist. From the people, my clients, to whom I've given care, I have also, in turn, received care. I've benefited from their wise sayings, gifts, and care for me.

One of my clients, Alice, who has since passed away, comforted me when I was burdened and troubled by a mistake I had made. I was tormented by what I thought was a terrible lapse in judgment. During a visit, Alice sensed that something was wrong; apparently I wasn't my usual self.

"Whatever is bothering you, learn from it," she said. Then she offered some gentle words, "Just don't let a bee sting you in the same place twice."

Bertha, who was over one hundred years old, was legally blind and fiercely independent. Once I got very angry with her paid caregiver because I felt that she was disabling Bertha by feeding her. I assumed that the caregiver was feeding her.

"She was only helping me with a napkin to protect my dress," Bertha said, correcting my assumption. Then she said, "Remember, if you get hungry enough, you'll find your mouth!"

It was another lesson for the caregiving journey. Allow the loved one their independence. There's often the capacity to find one's mouth, even with a "dis-ability." As a caregiver, don't interfere with a loved one's self-reliance.

My father was a jokester and playful. He was an extrovert who loved attention and knew ways to get it. (He was the youngest of his siblings and his mother's favorite, I think.) My father was a consummate manipulator; he knew just how to get his way.

One time, I found his caregiver feeding him when he could feed himself. I had given specific instructions to the caregiver to have my father do all that he could manage, but his skill at manipulation was in full play. Annoyed and peeved at my father and the caregiver, I asked the caregiver why she was feeding my father. She shrugged her shoulders sheepishly and said that my father asked her to feed him. I turned to my father, perplexed and angry with both of them.

"What's going on here?" I shouted.

My father said, "Why feed yourself, if you can get someone else to feed you?" He then winked at me and went into a fit of laughter. As a caregiver, it is so easy to be manipulated by the person who needs care. Be giving, but be wise and alert.

Once I was called to the bedside of a woman who was about my age. She was in the hospital. I don't remember her name. Before meeting a person who needs care or comfort, I learn as much about their history, attributes, cultural background, and personality as is possible. I had learned that this woman was a person of faith.

I entered her room where she was surrounded by her children. I greeted her and she responded. I sensed that there was an expectation for me to say or do something. I surprised myself by starting to sing the hymn, "Blessed Assurance, Jesus Is Mine." And I'm far from having a pleasant singing voice, but it didn't seem to matter to anyone, especially the woman I was visiting. I had never imagined myself singing as an act of caregiving. Her hospital room filled with soft cries. I, too, found myself crying. The woman looked at me and then turned to her loved ones, who all had tears in their eyes, and said, "Y'all stop worryin' and cryin' 'bout me. I'm all prayed up." Despite being near death, she still gave care to those of us who had surrounded her hospital bed.

I've had favorite clients along the way. It is hard not to. Nelson was one of my favorites. He was sitting on the edge of his bed in the rehab center when I first met him, arms folded over his chest with defensive body language that I read immediately. Nelson was not at all welcoming, nor had I expected him to be. His brother had warned me that Nelson was a handful and would likely not be receptive to my visit. With a smile and outstretched hand, I introduced myself and told him that his brother asked me to meet him. I knew I had to let Nelson know right away that I was on his side. So I asked with words carefully chosen, "What on earth are you doing in this place?" I deliberately emphasized *you* and *this place.*

Immediately, Nelson relaxed, unfolded his arms, and apparently sensed that I was not an agent of *this place.* I asked a few follow-up questions to learn what was what. Nelson had been pegged as a ripe candidate for long-term nursing care after rehab, and the nursing home had begun to set him up for a permanent stay—along with his money! From my experience working with hospitals and rehab facilities, I knew that it had already been documented that Nelson's living situation at home alone was not what is called a "safe and appropriate discharge." Nelson was financially solvent. He owned a two-million-dollar home in an upscale neighborhood. He was ripe for the picking for a long-term nursing home stay. He could pay privately. Knowing the underside of long-term care facilities and nursing and rehab centers, I asked Nelson if he had signed any documents.

"No," he said. "The only thing that I signed was a check to this place for $3,000."

Nelson had been at the rehab center for only a few weeks. He had been discharged from the hospital with recommendations for physical and occupational therapy. His rehab should have been covered by Medicare; there should have been no reason for him to have been asked to write a check for any amount. I began snooping by asking questions that received no answers. The trigger for an immediate transfer out of the facility was when I reviewed Nelson's rehab chart. It contained all the required documentation, language—"patient walked twenty feet"—but the telltale sign that exposed a mischarting of information was his demographic information. He was listed as African American; he was not.

Nelson authorized me to review his hospital records. I did not find anything conclusive, although there had been repeated hospitalizations and emergency room visits. With some background information about Nelson, I proposed a plan of care to which he agreed.

"Let's get you out of this place," I remember saying to him.

I took Nelson to visit several assisted living communities. I was surprised by what aspects of each place appealed to him and what didn't. Our visits gave me valuable insight about him and he got to know me.

Nelson selected an assisted living community that was about one mile from his house. He was a well-known figure in his old neighborhood. He was eccentric—his clothes, his habits, his personality, and his daily routine. Nelson thought that living in an assisted living community that was close to his old neighborhood would be great. Nelson's daily walks to the local library were well-known. He read the daily newspapers: the *Wall Street Journal*, the *New York Times*, and the *Washington Post*.

"All free," he would say, with a chuckle.

He was a fixture at several neighborhood restaurants. Nelson never cooked, nor could he have, had he been so inclined. The kitchen, like the rest of his two-million-dollar house, was uninhabitable, due to delayed maintenance and hoarding.

Something unexpected happened at the assisted living community. Nelson loved being there and decided to stay. He never returned to his house and simply turned things over to me to empty his house and arrange for its sale. Nelson had not attended to any estate matters, so the first step was to get him to an elderlaw attorney. Nelson hadn't given anyone power of attorney for health or finances, nor did he have a will or a trust. I was the only person Nelson had given any kind of authorization for anything. Fortunately, he liked and trusted the attorney and his affairs were put in order. Nelson collected ancient coins and was widely known for his collection. His numismatic interest, however, did not include sorting or organizing his collection, which was housed in two banks and multiple safe deposit drawers. I did some research and presented options to Nelson for selling his collection. He told me to manage the sale through a trusted rare coin dealer he had known for years. Eldercare can involve unusual tasks.

The plan of care for Nelson's first year in assisted living was to drill down for a diagnosis. I took him to see several specialists, with repeated visits. Finally, Dr. Frederick Barr, an oncologist in Bethesda, Maryland, determined that Nelson had acute myeloid leukemia. Nelson trooped through weeks and years of chemo. Yet, he loved going for chemotherapy. There, like elsewhere, Nelson got lots of attention from the nurses because he was benignly puckish and got away with a lot. Once I told him that in these times, men needed to be careful about what they said to a woman and how they behaved toward a woman because behavior and statements could be misconstrued or misinterpreted.

"Never mind," he would say. Nelson was playful and relational, but never inappropriate. Somehow the nurses at the infusion center seemed to know he was harmless. They reciprocated by giving him cookies and treats, which only increased his joy of going to the infusion center for chemo.

Nelson never called me "Irene." Instead, he called me "Commander-in-Chief." One Thanksgiving, I invited him for dinner in our home. It was a way that I took up caregiving as ministry. We incorporated Nelson into our family. Even though he declared that he was an agnostic, he was always respectful of and interested in Enrique's ministry. He enjoyed music, especially jazz, and attended our son's gigs when his group performed in Washington, DC.

After Nelson was diagnosed, I was poised for him to die from leukemia fairly quickly. I did the research. The five-year survival rate for adults was 24 percent. No one knew how long Nelson had had leukemia. Before I became involved with his care, he had not been seen by any doctor his entire adult life. For his cancer, Nelson was given Vidaza, one of the drugs of choice for his type of leukemia. Months, then years passed and except for the lethargy that lasted only a day after a chemo session, Nelson had a quality of life that we all deserve.

Nelson died suddenly, but not from leukemia.

I got a call that I should come right away to the emergency room. I knew the emergency room ropes. Identify yourself. Get a badge. Sign in. Be escorted to the person's emergency room cubicle. But this time things were different. Instead of being taken to Nelson's cubicle, I was led to a private room where I was met by a chaplain.

"How are you related to Mr. Butter?"

I mumbled, "What?" and my body nearly gave way.

Before I could even recover from the words "passed away," the chaplain said, "I am sorry. Mr. Butter aspirated. He was eating lunch and choked to death."

Even our best laid plans do not prepare for every contingency. Nelson had a wide circle of friends who turned out for his memorial service.

Let me share an adage that sustains me. I have borrowed the saying from a sorority sister's mother. Margie, my sorority sister, grew up in the South with eight siblings. Her family was devoutly Christian. Her parents worked diligently on their farm and educated all nine children. Margie's mother had a saying: "Stay ready, so you don't have to get ready," which I have embraced in my life. I've passed the saying along to everyone who knows me, including the individuals and families that I serve.

I will never be sure exactly what Margie's mother meant by the saying, but I have an idea. It's my guess that she meant we should stay ready by being steadfast in faith. There is a spiritual from the African American religious song tradition that may have inspired her words. The spiritual speaks to being ready when God calls us from our earthly home to the heavenly one:

I want to be ready, I want to be ready, and I want
    to be ready
 to walk in Jerusalem, just like John.[8]

---

8. From the African American spiritual "I Want to Be Ready," also called "Walk in Jerusalem." Public domain.

Each one of us will encounter eldercare in some form, expected or unexpected, directly or indirectly. We can't escape it. Current data assert that one in four families is impacted by eldercare needs. My guess is that the ratio is much higher—as much as four out of four, whether directly or not; whether a neighbor, a friend, a member of our family of origin, or an adopted or surrogate family member. Eldercare touches each one of us.

Stay ready.